Double-headed: More Tales from the Footplate

Colin G. Maggs

Sutton Publishing

First published in the United Kingdom in 2002 by
Sutton Publishing Limited · Phoenix Mill
Thrupp · Stroud · Gloucestershire · GL5 2BU

British Library Cataloguing in Publication Data
A catalogue record for this book is available from the British Library.

ISBN 0-7509-2815-8

Typeset in 11/13pt Bembo.
Typesetting and origination by
Sutton Publishing Limited.
Printed and bound in England by
J.H. Haynes & Co. Ltd, Sparkford.

CONTENTS

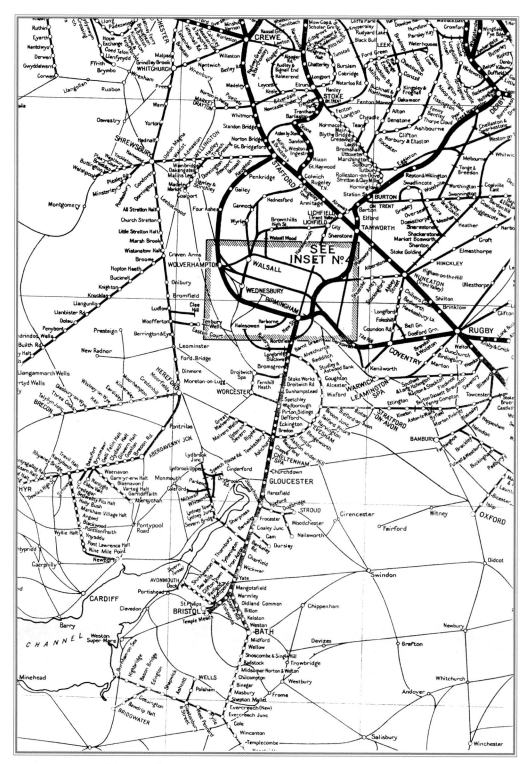

LMS map of the route from Crewe and Derby to Bristol and Bath, 1939. See page 7 for inset.

INTRODUCTION

I was greatly privileged to know two footplatemen who were excellent raconteurs and it is interesting to compare and contrast their experiences.

I first met Bob Ford in my doctor's waiting room, when I overheard him relating his railway experiences to another patient. Naturally I had a word with him and managed to secure an invitation to his home. It then transpired that we had had parallel lives: at one time we lived only 200 yards from each other; we shared a number of friends; we were at the same school under the same headmaster, albeit at different times and one as a pupil and the other an assistant master; and at different periods we sang in the same church choir.

Right to left: Bill Bagnall; St John Ross Goff, executive committee member of the Associated Society of Locomotive Engineers & Firemen; Colin G. Maggs.
(*c.* 1992 Author's collection)

Class 5 4–6–0 No. 45430 in Aston shed.
(15.9.65 Revd Alan Newman)

Bob was born in Bath, and for most of his railway life worked between Bath and Birmingham but also made quite a few trips over the Somerset & Dorset. Owing to the irregularity of working hours caused by locomotive rosters, circumstances eventually made it desirable for him to retire from British Railways and take a job driving the shunting engine at Bath gas works – quite a contrast from being in charge of the 'Pines Express'.

I was recommended to Bill Bagnall by another driver. Bill, born and bred in the Midlands, started work at the London & North Western Railway's Aston shed just after the First World War and moved to Barrow Road shed, Bristol, about 1929, working there for the next forty years. He ended up driving diesel-electrics.

As far as possible I have checked that all the facts related here are accurate, but it is just possible that Bob's and Bill's memories could have played them a few tricks.

Special thanks are due to R.B. Ireland for further checking and improving the text.

Chapter One

AT THE FOOT OF THE LADDER

B
ill Bagnall was born in Birmingham in a Peter Walker public house called the Wrexham after the brewer's headquarters. He then moved with the family to another hostelry, the Mint, but then, owing to his father's ill-health and subsequent death, the family moved to a private house in Aston. Every evening after school and all day Saturdays, he worked as a baker's errand boy (and later for the Public Boot Benefit Society), receiving 3*s* a week.

In 1915 he passed the Labour Exam. This meant that he could leave school aged 13 because he could say his 12 times table, calculate in decimal and common fractions, had attended metalwork or woodwork classes, and studied science. Then followed an assortment of jobs including making electric fans and working as a press operator and heating assistant to a hot stamper. After a period of unemployment in 1918, in April 1919 he secured a position on the London & North Western Railway, where extra staff had to be taken on after the introduction of the 8-hour day. Bill believed that being fatherless gave him an advantage over other applicants – certainly when he started as an engine cleaner at Aston on £2 2*s* a week he found himself among several other orphans. Everyone was quickly made aware that 'work' meant carrying out instructions issued by their immediate superior.

Aston motive power depot was situated by a junction which had four running lines to New Street and two to Stechford (forming a link for an alternative route between Rugby and Stafford in the event of a blockage on the Trent main line). There was also the Sutton line, an alternative between Wichnor Junction and New Street station. Aston shed, coded No. 10, opened in the mid-1880s and had twelve straight roads and an outside 42 ft-diameter turntable. Following normal LNWR practice, the water tank formed the roof of the coal stage. The locomotive stud comprised approximately sixty engines, mainly for freight duty. When Bill joined the shed staff, about 250 sets of men operated from it, including a ten-set Special Link which provided spare cover for the area. One driver, Teddy Morse, enjoyed an extensive route knowledge and had been known to reach Crewe North shed on a Monday and work from there until the following Sunday.

During the course of the next seven years Bill cleaned engines, and unloaded and stacked coal because the LNWR would purchase coal when the price fell and stack it for use when the price rose. When it did, Bill assisted in breaking the stack and loading the coal. Although hard work, it gave Bill and his colleagues useful experience in the use of shovel and pick. They also began to appreciate the different types of coal. Coal shifting also meant a little extra in Bill's wage packet – actually a tin in those days.

On another occasion Bill spent some months as a mate with Jointmaker Ketteridge. This taught him quite a lot about the construction of a locomotive. In those days the smokebox

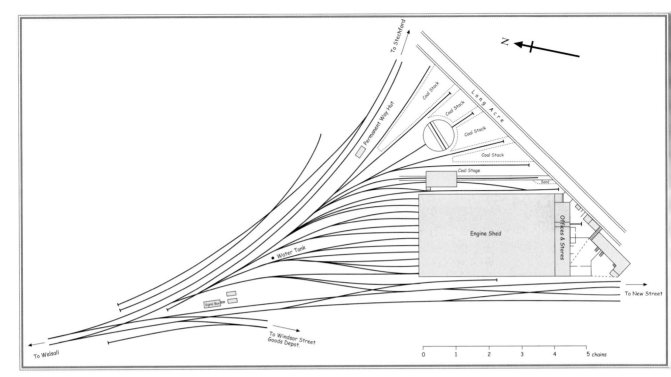

Plan of Aston Motive Power Depot, 1930.

doors needed to be packed with asbestos rope. Yards of it were hammered into a slot round the door to make it as air-tight as possible, for if air was drawn in it would impair an engine's steaming ability by reducing the amount of vacuum in the smokebox which is necessary for good combustion in the firebox. Bill recalled going to the stores one morning for the third time, with all the self-importance of an 18-year-old and demanding 'Five yards of smokebox door packing'. Storekeeper Teddy Brotch, trying to teach him politeness, said, 'If what?' Quick as a flash Bill impertinently replied, 'If you've b—— well got any!' As he spoke, he caught a glimpse of the boss's trilby hat, its owner just out of sight warming his backside by the storeman's fire. Wisely Bill made a very rapid retreat.

Bill also spent some time acting as a Call Boy. This entailed being responsible for seeing that every driver and fireman who had to sign on between midnight and 7.00am was roused by knocking at their door an hour beforehand. Additional lads were used to supplement the shift call boy at night, as he could not possibly manage to visit personally all the men involved. This employment enabled Bill's errand-boy knowledge of Birmingham to be further extended, reaching out to Dunlop's new factory at Fort Dunlop. He even became acquainted with the Lozells and Handsworth areas, though few men were able to persuade the District Locomotive Superintendent Mr Firkin to let them live that far from the shed. Calling up was important because if a driver or fireman missed his rostered turn three times, he lost his job and was reduced in grade. Thus, whenever a man was late, the call boy was immediately summoned to the Running Shift

No. 8814, a 4–6–0 '19-inch' Goods engine shedded at Birkenhead.
(*c.* 1934 Colin Roberts collection)

Foreman's office and asked 'Have you made the necessary knocking up?' The police, frequently seen on the streets in those days, soon got to know the call boys and would often offer assistance if needed.

One night Bill Lewis, the Locomotive Running Shift Foreman, knew that a particular 4–6–0 '19-inch Goods' engine needed a new brick arch fitted before it could be lit up. Steve Timms was the only man at that shed with the necessary skill but he worked a day shift. Unable to find another suitable engine, the foreman decided to call Timms out. Bill was detailed to find Steve's address. A call boy mainly used the footplate staff address book kept in the small office, but to find Steve's address, Bill had to go to the larger office to consult the 'general address book'. He discovered that Steve lived at a complicated address: No. 6, back of No. 2, Court 4, New Summer Street, off Summer Lane. It was situated in a very rough area of Birmingham.

Bill reached New Summer Street on his bicycle and on the corner saw a sergeant and a constable and asked them if they knew the location of Court 4. The sergeant said that the courts were numbered from the nearest end, odd numbers on the left and even on the right. Bill replied: 'Then I'll want the fourth one up on the right, eh?' Asked by the sergeant why he was going there, Bill answered: 'To find No. 6, back of No. 2, to call up Steve Timms so that he can build a brick arch in a "19-inch".'

The sergeant gave the constable a knowing look and told him: 'Show him the court entrance, but go no further'. As Bill and the constable proceeded, the officer inquired,

Ex-LNWR 0–6–2T No. 7740 temporarily in store at Bescot shed with its chimney covered, no coupling rod and a buffer missing. Part of the vacuum brake pipe is stored in the bunker. This locomotive was not withdrawn until June 1948.
(9.5.36 Colin Roberts collection)

'What's this lark about a 19-inch brick arch?' Bill explained its purpose and that '19-inch' referred to the size of the cylinders on a particular type of engine. 'You learn something every day on this job,' the constable replied.

When they reached the fourth entry Bill went on alone, pausing at a rank of eight houses – four in front with a central entrance to four at the rear. Bill passed through this archway and went to the door of what he calculated to be No. 6. As there was no knocker, he struck it with his hand. 'What's up?' came a cry from within. In reply Bill posed the question, 'Is this where Steve Timms lives?' Steve himself then thrust his head from the bedroom window only 8ft above the ground as Bill said, 'Steve, it's me, Baggy. They want you to come and put an arch in a "19-inch".' 'Hang on,' he called back. Once downstairs, he lit the gas lamp and invited Bill in, and was told about other cleaners having to fulfill the roster callings while Bill located him. Steve laughed and said, 'This is the first time in the years I've been on the job that I've had to be called out.' When Bill said, 'The copper that helped me find your court took a bit of convincing that it was a genuine request,' Steve commented. 'I'll bet he never entered the entry; they'll only come up there in daylight and in a crowd.' As Steve and Bill made their way to the street, they spied the two policemen on the corner; as Bill passed one said, 'You found him then.' Out of sight of the law, Bill put Steve on the crossbar of his bike and took him to the locomotive shed.

One day the Cleaner Foreman heard Bill yodelling to the rafters – the acoustics of the twelve-road shed certainly encouraged singing – and tried, unsuccessfully, to get him to join the church choir.

Bob Ford, a teenager living on the outskirts of Bath, was more interested in flesh and blood horses than in iron horses. He used to ride one animal to the blacksmith's leading a further three cart-horses, and one of his best friends was the farrier's son. Bob's first job on leaving school was as a delivery boy pushing a baker's handcart. His next step was to mechanical transport when he drove a Ford 8hp van belonging to another baker.

In his spare time he played football with other lads. Several of them worked on the railway, and told him that he would receive higher wages if he, too, worked on the line. This set Bob thinking. He liked the smell of steam and the character of railwaymen. He arranged to see A.H. Whitaker, LMS shedmaster at Bath and son of the former Somerset & Dorset Joint Railway's Locomotive Superintendent. This led to Bob having an eye test and being given an appointment to see the company's doctor in Pulteney Street. Little time was wasted and a few days later he received a brief letter: 'Commence duty at Walsall, Ryecroft Motive Power Depot, 18th September 1936'. A travel warrant was enclosed.

Carrying a suitcase containing, among other things, some brand new overalls, Bob went to Bath LMS station and caught the 8.30am local train to Mangotsfield, there passing through the dark and dank subway which inspired Arnold Ridley, also a Bath man, to write *The Ghost Train*. Reaching the Up main line platform, Bob caught the Bristol to Birmingham express. Who should be in the compartment he chose but two more Bath men, the brothers Gordon and Cliff Richards, both jockeys, going to Wolverhampton to ride. He left them at New Street, inquired the platform for Walsall and boarded the train indicated. It went at express speed and, as it flashed through a station, Bob saw 'Coventry' on a sign. He became alarmed. After half-an-hour a ticket collector came along and informed him that the train was actually bound for Euston non-stop; accepting Bob's explanation that he had been directed to the wrong platform, when they reached Euston the ticket collector kindly put him on a return train which left about ten minutes after his arrival. Back at New Street Bob had learned his lesson and asked a dozen people the correct platform for Walsall.

Finally arriving there, he asked the engine driver where the shed was. Replying 'Hop on', he drove him to the shed on his Webb '18-inch' 0–6–2T, Bob arriving in fine style. The driver left the engine over a pit for someone else to dispose and took Bill to Foreman Wheeler, kindly explaining to him the reason for the late arrival. He was then taken to his lodgings where there were four other lads from Bath.

Bill received £1 16s a week as a cleaner and from this he paid £1 a week for lodging and a shilling for having his overalls washed. Bill looked forward to earning £2 17s as a passed cleaner, but would only be paid permanently at that rate after he had spent 313 days (a year of six-day weeks) as a fireman. Clocking on at 8.00am, Bob cleaned engines until 4.00pm.

Ryecroft principally provided motive power for passenger trains, and engines Bob recalled were Fowler Class 3P 2–6–2T Nos 9, 11, 16, 17, 18, 26, 45, 54 and 69, also Nos 101, 104 and 154 which were Stanier versions of the same type. Stanier 2–6–0s

Bath LMS station, looking towards the buffers. On the right a Johnson Class 1P 0–4–4T heads a train to Mangotsfield and Bristol, while on the left is a train to Bournemouth West.
(*c.* 1930 Author's collection)

Driver's view from the cab of an Ivatt Class 2 2–6–2T by the bridge over the Avon west of Bath Green Park station.
(1963 W.F. Grainger)

Mangotsfield station, the view Down. Bob Ford travelled to Walsall from the platform on the right.
(*c.* 1960 Lens of Sutton)

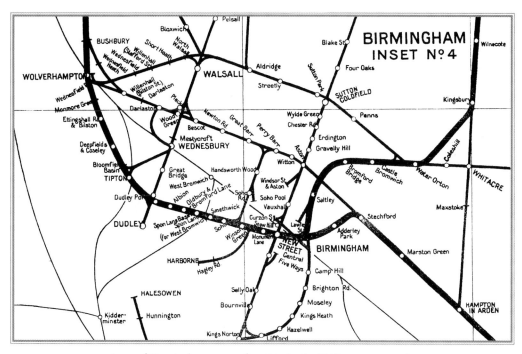

Inset of Birmingham area, referred to in the LMS map on page iv.

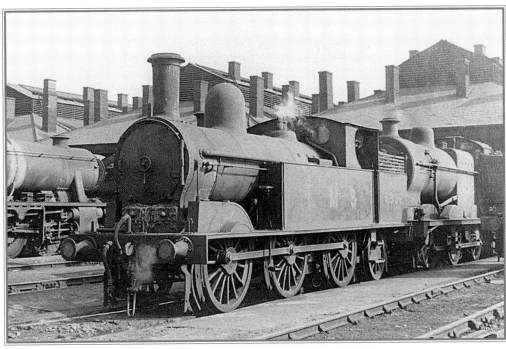

Webb '18-inch' 0–6–2T No. 6936 at Willesden shed.
(24.3.45 Colin Roberts collection)

Nos 2982 and 2984 were called 'The Moguls' to distinguish them from Hughes's 'Crabs' of the same wheel arrangement. The latter were equipped with American Detroit lubricators with about eight sight feeds. The vacuum pump was slung on the right-hand side of the engine beneath the cylinders and worked off the crosshead arm to avoid, supposedly, using the ejector, but in practice Bob found this unsatisfactory and the ejector had to be used. The shed also had some freight locomotives, these being 'Austin Seven' Fowler 0–8–0s and G1 class 0–8–0s No. 8913 and No. 9230, the G1s and G2s being commonly known as 'Super Ds'. Pride of the shed were 'Jubilee' class 4–6–0s, No. 5603 *Solomon Islands* and No. 5604 *Ceylon*. Bob and his mates were required to red wax their boiler cladding until it shone like silk; brass paste was used to clean the lining, while the motion was polished with emery cloth and then Vaselined. Tallow was applied to the tender sides and Yankee oil was used for washing axle boxes, brake hangers and wheels. On one occasion 'Black Five' 4–6–0 No. 5263 from another shed was prepared for the royal train. The cab's interior was white-washed, and its buffers emery-clothed; eight lads cleaned her for a week, even though she was virtually clean after one day.

The ex-London & North Western Railway shed at Ryecroft was typical of those built in the late 1870s. It was designed to accommodate a total of forty-eight locomotives on its twelve straight roads. As LNWR shed No. 9, it was responsible for a small sub-shed at Dudley and a signing-on point at Hednesford. Coded 3C by the LMS in 1935, it received a modern coal and ash plant in 1937 and new offices the following year. It had a

Class 2P 4–4–0 No. 40519 of 17B (Burton) shed, at Walsall, Ryecroft motive power depot.
(25.6.57 Revd Alan Newman)

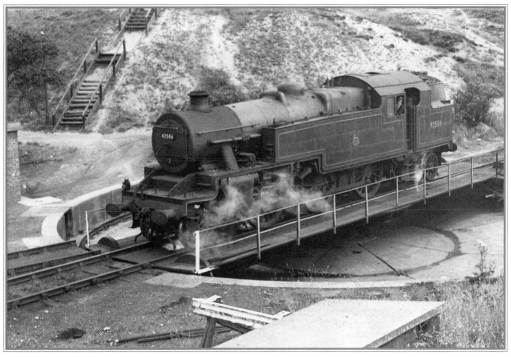

Stanier Class 4 2–6–4T No. 42586 on the turntable at Ryecroft shed.
(25.6.57 Revd Alan Newman)

Fowler Class 3P 2–6–2T No. 16.
(*c.* 1938 Author's collection)

Stanier Class 3P 2–6–2T No. 92 at Derby in ex-works condition. Notice the coal stack on the right.
(23.8.38 Revd Alan Newman)

Stanier Class 3P 2–6–2T No. 40174 at Newton Meadows, west of Bath, with the 11.35am Bristol St Philip's
to Bournemouth West.
(9.4.49 Author)

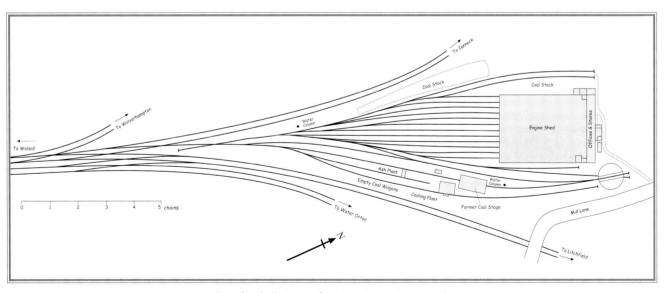

Plan of Walsall, Ryecroft Motive Power Depot, 1939.

Hughes/Fowler Class 5 'Crab' 2–6–0 No. 42707 of 2E (Saltley), at Barrow Road shed, Bristol.
(1963 W.F. Grainger)

Stanier Class 5 2–6–0 No. 42979 at Barrow Road.
(*c.* 1963 W.F. Grainger)

Fowler 'Austin Seven' Class 7F 0–8–0 No. 9569.
(*c.* 1938 Colin Roberts collection)

60ft-diameter turntable, a disposal siding and a back stage road, the latter being used for coaling by hand when the hopper broke down. When this happened the lads were paid 4½*d* a ton for coaling a tender from a low-sided wagon, the rate increasing to 6*d* from a high-sided wagon. Each youth shifted 40 tons a night for a fortnight, thus earning £6 a week.

The shed toilet consisted of six pews of 12ft-long planks situated over a cesspit, each pew accommodating four or five men. Despite the use of disinfectant, which looked like red sand, it was a smelly place and took some getting used to; nevertheless men sat there reading newspapers and talking.

Bob cleaned engines at Ryecroft for three months and was then taken to the time office to meet Driver Archie Goode, about 40 years of age, rotund and jovial. Bob accompanied him to his 'Super D', checked the coal, trimmed the lamps and moved off shed to Norton hill to work on the 'Humpy' – the hump marshalling yard where shunting went on continuously. The engine had to be fired left-handedly and this was made more awkward as the footplate was so confined. The firehole door went up inside

'Super D' Class 7F 0–8–0 No. 9436.
(*c.* 1936 Author's collection)

'Super D' Class 7F 0–8–0 No. 9092 at Bushbury shed. On the left is Webb '18-inch' 0–6–2T No. 6987.
(4.7.36 S.W. Baker)

Shed scene: 'Jubilee' Class 4–6–0 No. 5554 (later named *Ontario*), at Crewe with shed plate 2A (Rugby). An oilcan has been placed on the motion while the photograph was taken. Another can is on the ground.
(March 1935 Colin Roberts collection)

Shed scene: Class 2P 4–4–0 No. 563 of 22C (Bath) at Templecombe. To the right of the smokebox is a steam valve to which has been connected a flexible pipe which in turn is joined to a rigid pipe forming a steam lance to clean the tubes. The smokebox door is unclipped.
(5.5.49 Colin Roberts collection)

Shed scene: Cleaners at Barrow Road shed, Bristol. Front centre is Joe Hickmoth; back row, left to right: Jack Norton, -?-, Tommy Slipp, -?-, -?-, Alf Jones. The engine is probably Class 5 4–6–0 No. 5288.
(*c.* 1937 W. Jones collection)

Shed scene: Passed Fireman Walter Grainger at Bristol, Barrow Road, oiling the big end of a Class 4F 0–6–0 built at Derby in 1928.
(July 1962 W.F. Grainger)

No. 58343, an 0–6–0 'Coal Engine' at Crewe Works.
(17.5.51 Revd Alan Newman)

the firebox to act as a baffle plate so that cold air was deflected under the brick arch, thus avoiding damage to the tube plate which would result in leaking tubes.

The flat firebox, 10ft 6in in length, needed to be fired evenly round the box and to win best results the fire never exceeded 4in depth. One firing averaged 60lb of coal, that is, ten shovelfuls. When the engine was ready, sixty wagons were coupled on, and the engine drew round the hump and then pushed the wagons back slowly at 1mph, gravity taking them downhill, as shunters directed them into the appropriate siding. The fact that 'Super Ds' were free steamers made Bob's task lighter; he enjoyed firing and thought it an easy job. LNWR engines depended on blast and had a large chimney, pulling a lot of fire through their tubes; their smokebox doors sometimes had char inside to a depth of 16–17in. This made it very hot work.

Bob also fired on a shunter with Driver Richard Knight, who had had to leave main line duties because of failing eyesight and was rostered in the shunting link where he accepted no serious responsibility. He invariably sat on the fireman's seat and allowed Bill to drive as well as fire the Class 2F 0–6–0 'Coal Engine'. Bob had no problem maintaining the fire because there was no need to use more than 5 or 6cwt of coal

'Jubilee' Class 4–6–0 No. 5651 *Shovell* heads an express passenger train.
(*c.* 1938 Colin Roberts collection)

during an eight-hour shift for work was spasmodic – they might be busy for an hour and then stand stationary for another hour.

Next Bob was paired with a ginger-haired driver who had a reputation as rather a dictator, but they got on well and Bob liked No. 9521, a Fowler Class 7F 'Austin Seven' 0–8–0. Then one day Driver Len Allsop asked Bob to go to Wolverhampton, ride 'on the cushions' to Crewe and return with a special originating from Blackpool. Arriving at Crewe they waited and waited. Eventually 'Jubilee' class No. 5651 *Shovell*, with fifteen coaches, drew in very late, the brakes sounding as if they were dragging. The pressure gauge only registered 120lb – the maximum was 225lb – so something was seriously wrong. The locomotive inspector asked Bob to open the smokebox door, warning him to do it slowly. It was good advice, as the superheater element was blowing across the blast pipe, preventing the exhaust steam from creating a good draught and bringing plenty of oxygen to the fire. The inspector, realising that the engine was a failure, called back the crew going off duty and asked them to take the 'Jubilee' to the shed. A 'Black Five' standing by as station pilot was coupled to the train and express headlights fitted. Bob was not too worried about his responsibilities for Len had promised to look after him.

Fortunately the fire was already made up on the 'Black Five' and did not require much attention. Bob fired and she made plenty of smoke, but was found to be 'hanging', that is, not making steam. Len said: 'Put a dozen round her', but it wasn't enough and Bob had to fire almost continuously to maintain the steam pressure. He grew very tired and wondered whether he had chosen the right job. Approaching the Whitmore water-

Sister engine to No. 20008, this is Class 1P 2–4–0 No. 2 (originally MR No. 158 and renumbered 20002 in May 1934) at Barrow Road. It was withdrawn in July 1947 and is now preserved at the Midland Railway Centre. (1932 Colin Roberts collection)

troughs between Crewe and Stafford, Len said: 'Get it down' and Bob lowered the scoop. They picked up water all right – in fact they got too much! Lacking experience, Bob failed to raise the scoop quickly enough. The tender overfilled, the water tank lid blew open and water cascaded out, drenching the front coaches. Bob hoped there were no passengers looking out of the windows. They stopped at Wolverhampton, where they uncoupled, and then ran light engine to Ryecroft. On the disposal road Bob levelled the fire and found clinker on the firebars which had starved the fire of air. The engine had been standing ready at Crewe for 16 hours, during which time the fire had not been cleaned, and the reason why she failed to steam properly was because the air could not get through. Weeks later Bob made a trip all the way from Wolverhampton to Fleetwood and back on a good engine and found that firing was not such hard work after all.

One interesting engine at Ryecroft shed was No. 20008, which was painted red and driven by Archie Goodwin who had considerable knowledge of the LMS roads and could drive an inspection saloon almost anywhere. The Kirtley double-framed 2–4–0 No. 20008 had been built at Derby in June 1867 as No. 106 of the '156 Class'. As trains increased in weight, these relatively small machines became obsolete as express engines and most of the class had been withdrawn by 1933 when No. 20008 was reconditioned. In 1935 she became *Engineer Liverpool* and later the same year *Engineer Watford*, and from

'Jubilee' Class 4–6–0 No. 5641 *Sandwich* of 22A (Bristol) at Gloucester Eastgate with a Bristol to
Bradford express.
(June 1947 Roger Venning)

'Jubilee' Class 4–6–0 No. 5709 *Implacable* of 22A (Bristol) at Gloucester with a Birmingham to Bristol
stopping train. Class 4P Compound 4–4–0 No. 1036 is on the right, acting as station pilot.
(12.4.47 Roger Venning)

Class 5 4–6–0 No. 45263 of 2E (Saltley) at Barrow Road.
(19.11.64 Revd Alan Newman)

'Claughton' Class 4–6–0 No. 5946 *Duke of Connaught* at Crewe North. This engine was withdrawn in
February 1941.
(22.8.38 Revd Alan Newman)

Class 5 4–6–0 No. 5167.

(*c.* 1937 Author's collection)

1937 until 1942 she was *Engineer Walsall*. She was withdrawn in June that year. Also shedded at Ryecroft was an ex-LNWR 2–4–0 with wooden brake blocks on the tender wheels. Driven by Simeon Foster, she was scheduled to head an express over the 11 miles from New Street to Walsall in 19 minutes.

Teamed with Driver George Caldicott, Bob was placed in the Special Link at Walsall. It had sixteen passed firemen and sixteen passed cleaners and it was a roster link so they circulated round the sixteen jobs. One duty was called the 'Meat Train'. It had about twelve coaches and carried workers from Hednesford to Vauxhall & Duddeston. Leaving at 6.35am, it stopped at all stations. The 'Meat Train' was assigned a variety of engines: 'Jubilees', 'Black Fives', a Cooke 'Prince of Wales' 4–6–0 and the red 'Claughton' No. 6004. The latter was free steaming and competently mastered the twelve coaches.

Ryecroft shed was allocated three Fowler Class 4P 2–6–4 tank engines and a further three of Stanier's improved variety. Both types were very good engines capable of working a ten-coach express easily. In those days before rocking grates Bob vividly remembered the problems he experienced when trying to remove clinker with a 10ft-long shovel. Because of the length of the firebox and the relatively confined space within the cab, and despite opening the rat-trap latch door to the coal bunker, it was still quite a difficult task manoeuvring a shovelful of clinker out of the box to deposit the clinker on the ash heap. It entailed having the handle protruding through the opening on the fireman's side of the cab and the blade projecting from the driver's side. The fact that the handle grew very hot, eventually even glowing red hot, only added to Bob's difficulties. He believed they were the most awkward engines to dispose of – in fact, contrary to regulations, it was not uncommon for a couple of fire bars to be taken up and the clinker shovelled through to the ashpan, the driver then getting underneath and raking it out. The driver used a hosepipe to spray water into the ashpan so that the choking, hot dust was immediately damped down and cooled, thus enabling him to rake it out immediately, leaving a perfectly clean ashpan and a perfectly clean grate.

Thus far Bob found the task tolerably easy and pleasant, but the job of replacing the set of bars was somewhat tricky. Those taken out were from the middle section of the grate and removal was easy. You simply took an iron rod with little twin hooks on and dropped it down over the bar; as the end of the bar was lugged, it was a simple matter to place the hooks below the lugs. Then you lifted and pulled – and the bar was out. It was lifted straight from the grate on to the footplate still red hot and left there to cool.

To replace the firebars, a rod with a small L-shaped end like a little pricker was used. The firebar was placed on the grate on its side, and then manoeuvred into the exact position (this operation being carried out at a distance of about 7ft from the person doing it). Once in the right place it was suddenly tipped so that it dropped into place. The bar was then pushed tightly against those left in. The second bar was then replaced in the same way and pushed against the others. The problem was the third bar, which was always a tight fit. The bearer where the bars rested had been cleaned free of ash and clinker in order to allow the bars to fall in flat. Once the third bar was almost in position, it was used like a hammer to make sure it sat flat and not proud.

One night Bob carried out this task on a 'Jubilee'. He had been on shed relief with the ginger-haired Jabe Cozens, a very good and competent passed fireman, and they had already disposed of six engines. When they came to the 'Jubilee', Jabe said, 'Bob, it's very hard work tonight, let's have the bars out of this engine. I don't like the thought of you shovelling all that lot out after what you've done already.' Bob, only 19 at the time, said, 'Well, all right, Jabe, I'll do whatever you say; you're the driver and she's certainly got a really dirty fire. We've had enough of clinker shovelling, I'll get the bars off.' So saying, he lifted three bars out.

Bob found it easy to push the clinker down through the gap in the firebars while Jabe, underneath in the pit, raked it all out. The fire cleaned, Jabe returned to the footplate. They fitted two of the bars back in easily, but the third would just *not* go in. And time was not on their side. It was now after 4.00am and the 'Jubilee' was scheduled to be going out on a job soon after 7.00am, so that bar just had to be replaced. Jabe was ultimately responsible as he had instructed Bob to take the bars out. But Jabe did not want any trouble with the foreman if the engine was not ready to leave on time, so he told Bob to lift out the baffle plate. He duly took it out on the shovel and threw it back towards the tender. The baffle plate, normally placed in the upper part of the firehole,

Fowler Class 4P 2–6–4T No. 2313 *The Prince*. This engine was under construction at Derby when HRH the Prince of Wales visited the works on 28 February 1928. By 1933 the name had been painted out.
(*c.* 1928 Author's collection)

Stanier Class 4 2–6–4T No. 2444.
(*c.* 1938 Author's collection)

Fowler Class 4 2–6–4T No. 42307 at Shrewsbury. On the left is No. 5025 *Chirk Castle*.
(16.8.60 Revd Alan Newman)

Fowler Class 4 2–6–4T No. 2387 and Fowler Class 3 No. 15509 at Derby.
(28.5.33 Colin Roberts collection)

The cab of an LMS Stanier 4–6–0. A boilersmith is entering or leaving the firebox.
(1936 Author's collection)

was designed to direct air down towards the firebed in order to mix it thoroughly with the hot gases and flames to improve combustion and maximise heat from the coal.

There was a fire with about a hundredweight of coal in the box. Jabe took a couple of wipers, took hold of the protector plate and lifted it out from the bottom of the firehole. Bob had never seen one removed before – he thought it was shaped like false teeth. Jabe removed his overall slop and gave Bob his cap. Then he grabbed a wiper, dipped it into a bucket of water and placed the wet wiper over his face to help him breathe inside that hot firebox. Jabe told Bob to check if there was anyone about. There wasn't, so Jabe wriggled into the firebox, pushed the obstinate bar down in place and was out again in about 40 seconds, sweating profusely because of the intense heat. Then he put on his slop and overcoat while Bob cleaned the char from the smokebox. Bob vividly remembered Jabe going into that firebox because he was the only other person there and if something had gone wrong and Jabe had died, Bob would have been in serious trouble, even though he was only a fireman and had to obey his driver's instructions.

Bob knew from experience what it was like to be stuck in a firebox because he had been trapped in one himself, though fortunately it was only a cold one. When he tried to come out, he found that his shoulders would not go through the firehole. 'If you get hot you swell and if you panic you swell,' Bob was told by the man in with him. 'Put your hands above your head, kid, right up. Push your hands out and I'll push up your feet.' Bob obeyed and popped out as easily as a cork from a bottle. Putting his arms up made his shoulders less broad and he was a more streamlined shape to slip through the hole. Bob now knew why the bars were not supposed to be taken out. If an engine was going into traffic within three to four hours, the process of fire cleaning was supposed to happen like this. The dampers were shut and the engine placed over a pit with perhaps 140–150lb of steam, that is, something like 50lb below normal, and with the boiler full of water. A bent dart, which was an iron with an arrow-shaped head, was pushed down under the door and the clinker pushed forward, clearing the back of the box of everything. Then, using a clinker shovel, any clean fire was taken off the top of the clinker; by withdrawing the shovel and turning it over, the clean fire was dropped under the firehole door. There might be half a dozen to a dozen shovelfuls. Next, a couple of dozen lumps of fresh coal were put on top of the fire to catch alight.

All the clinker was now at the front of the box. The fireman then took a straight dart and ran it down the remaining bars to break off the clinker which sometimes formed plates 1in thick and 2–3ft in diameter. If possible it was broken into convenient sizes for disposal, but sometimes it was very hard and difficult to break. Then, again using the clinker shovel, the rest of the box was cleared out completely, leaving the coal burning beneath the door. When the fire had been cleaned, the engine would be taken into the shed and handed to the steam raiser, who kept it with about 100lb head of steam and a small fire under the door so that when she was required, the fire could be built up and sufficient steam raised for working a train within an hour or so. If the boiler was due for a washout, or the engine was required to go into the shed dead, then the disposal crew were allowed to pull the bars up and drop all the fire.

Chapter Two

BOB FORD RETURNS TO BATH

One day Bob heard that a Walsall man based at Bath wanted to return home. As he had about the same seniority as Bob they applied for exchange and were successful in having it approved. Bob started at Bath motive power depot, LMS code 22C, on 5 January 1939, but he was not given much firing until June.

Bath was quite a contrast to Walsall. Bath was busiest in summer, whereas Walsall was busier in winter when coal traffic was greater. Bath was really only ticking over until about April and then in the summer half of the year excursions were put on and more men were required for footplate work. Sometimes as many as sixteen extra trains were run to Bournemouth, which meant that thirty-two men were required. Sixteen passed firemen would be split from their normal drivers and these drivers given a replacement mate. The passed firemen also required a mate and these were found from the ranks of the cleaners. In 1939 Bath MPD had forty passed firemen and about sixty registered firemen and passed cleaners.

There were two engine sheds at Bath. The stone-built Midland shed beside the main line was erected in about 1869, while the coming of the Somerset & Dorset Railway in 1874 saw the construction of a timber-built two-road shed, an identical two-road side extension being added three years later. This S&D shed measured approximately 300ft by 60ft, the four roads terminating at immense wooden stop blocks. Some ten or twelve timber columns supported the beams below the roof centre and each track had a pit the length of the shed. Necessary fire precautions among the flammable material consisted of boiler washing-out hoses and numerous buckets of water hanging on the shed walls.

Progression of a Footplateman

Cleaner
Passed cleaner (i.e., passed for firing duty)
Fireman
Registered fireman (i.e., covered a minimum of 313 firing turns)
Passed fireman (i.e., passed for driving duty)
Driver
Registered driver (i.e., covered a minimum of 313 driving turns)

Bath Motive Power Depot seen from the top of the water softener. The timber-built Somerset & Dorset
shed is towards the left, and the stone-built Midland shed on the right. A Class 3F 0–6–0T is shunting empty
wagons from the coal stage. An express is leaving, headed by two 4–4–0s.

(1938 Author's collection)

Both companies shared the turntable, a new one of 60ft diameter being installed in
1935.

An unusual feature at Bath was the 'Boat Road' leading down between the loco depot
and the river to a shed that was originally used for the transfer of goods between rail and
barge. The heavy engineering firm of Stothert & Pitt exchanged about a dozen wagons
daily at the Boat Road into or out of traffic, the siding being shunted at about 4.30pm by
the engine working at the S&D sidings at Bath Junction, this locomotive taking on water
at the loco depot. When it came in it had worked for 24 hours and the new shift took
out a fresh engine.

Bob remembered some of the engines when he first arrived at the shed. There were
'Black Fives' Nos 5023, 5029, 5194, 5389, 5440 – considered the best of all – and 5448.
Of the eleven S&D Class 7F 2–8–0s, Nos 13806, 13807 and 13808 still had their original
G9BS boilers, 7in in diameter larger than the early locomotives of the class with standard

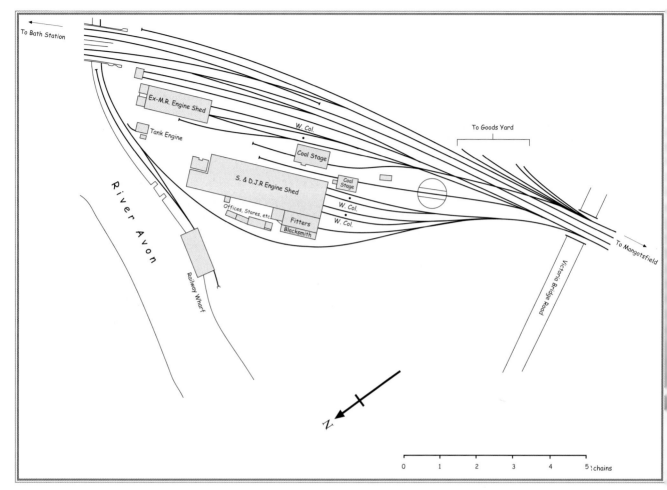

Bath Motive Power Depot, 1930.

G9AS boilers as fitted to the 4–4–0 Compounds. Compound No. 935 was ex-shops and in excellent condition, often taking the 'Pines Express' northwards out of Bath. 'Jubilee' No. 5626 *Seychelles* frequently appeared on this express while No. 5612 *Jamaica* was actually shedded at Bath and had a straight high-sided tender which looked rather ugly, especially as the cab was wider than the tender. One 'Crab' 2–6–0 had Caprotti valve gear and from mid-position needed three-and-a-half turns to full fore gear and one-and-a-half turns to reverse. It was equipped with a 'bacon slicer' regulator, the long handle capable of being pulled or pushed by both driver and fireman together.

Arthur Elliott and Tom Rugg were the running shed foremen and in the daytime Tom White was the loco superintendent and engineer. He had nothing to do with the running side and ordering men about, this being Fred Jefferies' job. At other depots there was always a foreman in charge to make decisions and instruct drivers on such matters as which pit to use for disposal, which road to put an engine on after disposal, and whether a locomotive was to go out to traffic again or should be stabled. This

Class 4F 'Armstrong' 0–6–0 No. 44523 and Class 7F 2–8–0 No. 13805 of 22C (Bath) at Bath. The overhead gantry is for carrying ash.

(15.8.49 Author)

Class 7F 2–8–0 No. 53801 of 71G (Bath) at Derby.

(19.11.55 Author's collection)

Large-boiler Class 7F 2–8–0 No. 90.
(1925 Author's collection)

'Jubilee' Class 4–6–0 No. 45612 *Jamaica* of 17A (Derby) at Bath shed. Class 7F 2–8–0 No. 53810 is on the
right. Note the gas lamp.
(*c.* 1960 R.J. Cannon/Author's collection)

knowledge was essential so that the crew would know whether the engine's fire should be completely disposed of or retained. For some reason Bath MPD was unusual, and Fred Jefferies, who was shed marshal, ran things as efficiently as a military manoeuvre. His post was known as the 'Seven o'clock loco' because that was the time he came on duty, and he stayed until 3.00pm each day. He was fortunate to have such pleasant hours, without the responsibility of working on the main line. It was also unusual in that he had a permanent position instead of being placed in a link. He had his own fireman and his own cabin by the water softener at the top of the slope leading down to the S&D shed.

When Bob arrived at Bath in January 1939 he had already done 313 turns of firing so was on his first rate of pay. As well as cleaning, quite often the foreman would delegate one of the cleaners to assist a shed labourer carrying out some task, or help the boilersmith. Doing these jobs gave Bob, quite literally, a deeper insight into locomotives. He helped one old fellow whose job was replacing brick arches in the fireboxes of engines that had been washed out, and where the arch was in a dilapidated or almost collapsed state. Bob went into the firebox with him and watched the man place a couple of steel bars up the sides of the firebox on two bolts positioned there for this purpose. He set a wooden rack between the bars to give support to the arch he was building. Bob brought in three barrow-loads of firebricks and the old man had a bucket of Purimachos, a fireclay that acted as a mortar capable of withstanding heat to white hot temperatures. In fact, the heat could even form 'icicles' but the clay would not collapse. They worked in the firebox together, Bob handing up the bricks which his mate placed in position after smarming on Purimachos. When the arch was completed, they removed the two bars and the arch remained firmly in place at the front of the firebox under the tube plate.

The purpose of the arch was to circulate the hot gases given off at the front of the fire and protect the firebox tube plate from the fierce heat of the fire. Unofficially, the brick arch had another purpose. If you were on an engine standing stationary and steaming poorly owing to a clinkered-up fire, it was unwise to clean it by dropping clinker on the ground because it might well start a blaze, or if it were at night a signalman, or someone, would have been sure to spot the hot clinker and believe it to be a fire. Providing you were standing for about half an hour or so, there was an alternative. Bob actually put sheets of clinker, perhaps as large as 15in by 12in, on top of the brick arch. He placed as many as a dozen shovelfuls there as it was the only place he could put it without stirring attention. Because of the slope of the arch, it was impossible to remove until someone climbed into the firebox at the next washout.

The LMS always ordered good coal from the pits and would not accept responsibility for poor coal. As a young fireman, Bob was taught how to avoid undue clinkering, especially with some of the inferior types of coal. When making up the fire on shed before going out into traffic, a dozen lumps of fire brick should be thrown on the firebox bars, these effectively preventing clinker from forming in sheets and thus stopping the air getting in.

Some footplatemen, through no fault of their own, were unable to work certain turns. Stan Shellard, one of the best firemen that ever picked up a shovel at Bath, developed varicose veins when he was aged about 40. It had such an effect on his health that he had

View through the Up Winsor Hill Tunnel to the signal box.
(31.7.59 Author)

to give up most of his link work and ended up as permanent fireman on the shunter or banker. This meant that he could never be out on the main line enjoying himself. Then there was Driver Art Riglin, who worked in the Midland passenger link for many years. He had a very bad accident when a superheater tube element split and the escaping steam damaged the firehole door. He was standing beside the door at the time and his right leg was very badly burned and scalded. Subsequently he only accepted local duties such as Bath–Bristol–Wickwar and when it was his turn to work the 'Pines Express' or the night parcel train to Birmingham and back, another driver in the link took it for him. Invariably Bob's driver took over Art's parcels duty and someone else his 'Pines' turn. When in that link Bob fired for Art for one week in every six while Bob's driver was working Art's parcels turn.

Then there was a fireman on the Bath shunting engine who had lost three fingers from one hand and had to be given a job he was able to cope with. He was made a permanent fireman on the shunter, but after fifteen years or so on this duty he was so frustrated that he committed suicide by jumping into the Avon at Pulteney Weir.

Another sad mishap occurred in about 1940. As the Down 'Pines Express' passed Masbury Summit, 811ft above sea level, the dampers were shut and the blower turned on. Passing through Winsor Hill Tunnel at about 60mph, there was a severe blow-back, and the fireman's hands and face being so badly burned that he was off duty for four to

No. 8714, a 4–6–0 '19-inch Goods'.
(*c.* 1927 Colin Roberts collection)

five months. The driver, fortunately, got off lightly – the plate that shielded his eyes from the fire kept the flames away from him. In order to prevent such a blow-back, it was standard practice that when a driver closed his regulator he automatically turned the blower on, and when a fireman shut a damper he always turned the blower on a little to make sure that the fire kept going through the tubes. It was believed that in this case the damper had not been closed properly.

As a cleaner passed for firing duties from Aston shed, Bill Bagnall found that the fifteen oldest men were carefully placed in the three-shift system: five in the 6.00am to 2.00pm shift; five from 2.00pm until 10.00pm; and five from 10.00pm till 6.00am. One day, when on the middle shift, Bill was asked for the very first time to report at 5.20pm for a double trip to London. On arrival at the shed he discovered his mate to be an elderly main line driver with a peculiar manner of speech, his nasal twang causing the cleaners to nickname him 'Moaner'.

When Bill reached the engine, a '19-inch' 4–6–0, Driver Pop Dowling was already there. Bill climbed on to the footplate and, glancing at the tender, remarked that it was full of Blaina – a Welsh coal with poor steaming characteristics. Dowling replied, 'We'll have to make the best of it'. Bill discovered that when he struck a lump with his coal pick, it was like hitting a wet sack, the lump often disintegrating into small slack which tended to prevent air getting into the fire. Bill did his best to create a fire by selecting a few hand-sized pieces and at intervals he placed on more. In this way he managed to build a reasonable fire for the start of the journey and in doing so worked up quite a sweat.

They travelled light engine to the loop at Stechford to pick up their train. As Bill passed above Washwood Heath Sidings, little did he think that in later years, between 1932 and 1936, he would pass below that viaduct when firing express passenger trains. Arriving at Stechford they backed on to their train. Most of the wagons were for Camden's Chalk Farm Sidings, but a few at the front had to be shunted off at Coventry.

Bill's misgivings about the steaming qualities of his coal soon proved to be true and he was soon 'dodging the door' – a practice whereby the driver opens and closes the firehole door for his fireman. This procedure ensured that less air entered the firebox above the fire and more was drawn through the fire from below, thus encouraging combustion. They ambled through Berkswell Tunnel and Tile Hill station and drew to a stop at Coventry. Unfortunately from the load point of view, they had to attach more wagons than they dropped, so the anticipated lighter load failed to materialise.

All the while 'Moaner' subjected Bill to a 'volume of nasal vituperation that was almost unbearable'. Nevertheless Bill remained quiet and did his best, but the poor-quality coal was easily beating him. As Bill ran up the coal to the back of the tender in order to take on water, his driver yelled at him. Now Bill himself was at boiling point, even if the water in the boiler was struggling to reach this temperature! Bill still managed to restrain his feelings.

As they passed over Holbrook Park water troughs their speed was so low that it was impossible to top up the water tank and they had to make a special stop at Rugby, with Moaner ranting on all the while. As they stopped by a water crane there, Bill asked, 'Ain't there a loco shed here?' 'Yes,' he replied. 'Why?' Then Bill really let fly. 'This is my first trip to London and I've done my best and all you've done is to moan at everything I've done and I've just had enough. I'm going over to that loco depot to ask them to send a fireman over to you. If this is the kind of job firing is, I've had my lot!'

Bill's outburst had the desired effect. 'Come here, you young sweep,' Moaner replied. 'We're Aston men and we must stick to the job, good or bad. I won't say another word. You carry on and do your best – no one can do more than that.'

They left Rugby and Bill, who had no experience of the road beyond, worked like a slave and managed generally to keep the steam pressure up, though they did have to stop at Roade to 'blow up'. Bill discovered subsequently that this was a favourite point for locomotives to rest and recover. Throughout the whole trip Bill failed to spot from the cab any lineside features, as his attention was focused solely on the steam gauge and the water level, these being his two prime concerns.

Eventually they reached Chalk Farm where they uncoupled from the train and ran light engine to Camden shed. There they signed off, went to the barracks and after a wash and a snack Bill sought his cubicle from the ninety there and as soon as he lay down 'went out like a light'. The next thing he knew was the barrack steward shaking him nine hours later.

In the wash room he met Jimmy Hough, an Aston main line fireman, who said: 'Hello Baggy, what on earth are you doing here?' Bill replied: 'I'm mating old Moaner and I ain't liking it a bit. We had words at Rugby and I threatened to leave him. We had Blaina coal; were short of steam most of the way and had to stop to blow up.' 'Well Baggy, you won't get Blaina coal here, it's a first-class shed and the bloke who directed any of that stuff here would soon lose his job.'

'I ain't a bit keen on the trip back whatever coal we have,' persisted Bill. 'Don't be afraid,' said Jimmy. 'If you've a tender of that shiny stuff, make sure you run the dart along the bars about every 20 miles to keep the air going through it. Also make sure that the front damper is shut before you leave the shed. If you have an "Experiment" class 4–6–0, the top lever is the damper control, so if your mate wants the cocks opened, make sure you use the bottom lever.' Grateful for the advice, Bill thanked him warmly. 'I'm pleased I've met you here and glad to have received the benefit of your experience. Thanks again.'

They did have an 'Experiment' and shiny coal, so Bill put Jimmy Hough's advice into practice and it worked like a charm. They left Chalk Farm with sixty-five wagons and a 2–4–0 in the front to assist to Northampton. When the pilot engine was taken off, Bill felt quite confident that he had mastered the job. Old Moaner even managed to burst into song and only once did he attempt to interfere and that was when Bill was about to 'run the dart down her'. He said to Moaner, 'Leave me alone, I know what I'm about,' and after that he was left to his own devices. By the time they reached Stechford goods yard Moaner said, 'If my usual mate ain't right for work next trip, I'll ask for you.' Bill replied, 'Well, I'd not relish the job after the way you treated me on the trip up.'

For some time afterwards, every time they met Moaner would ask, 'How goes it, you young shaver?' Bill believed he had struck a nerve by threatening to leave him that night at Rugby, and that Moaner had been impressed on the return trip when Bill performed to his satisfaction owing to the 'know-how' that a more experienced fireman had imparted. The Up trip proved to Bill that when working under difficult conditions a critical driver was more of a hindrance than a help.

Bob Ford said that as a registered fireman the first driver to whom he was linked was Sammy Randall, who told him about the days when he was a young fireman. Bob thought it must have been sheer murder. Each driver had his own engine that nobody else drove, and this made some men highly possessive. Sammy recalled that his driver drew a line down the centre of the footplate and warned him that this was his side and his side alone.

Bob said that if the 'handedness' of an engine did not suit you, or you were not lucky enough to be ambidextrous, it was difficult work because you had to fire against your natural instinct. Bob himself was a natural left-hander but he quickly learned to fire right-handed as well. Five of the Somerset & Dorset Class 7F 2–8–0s (Nos 13806 to 13810) were left-handers and six were right-handers (Nos 13800 to 13805). Drivers preferred their firemen to fire from their own side so that they did not feel congested, for footplates were generally far from spacious.

When Bob returned to Bath he discovered that most of the Dorset goods link drivers were old men unable to be promoted into passenger links because they lacked the road knowledge. Once they achieved the goods link at about 38 to 40 years of age they knew that they would remain there for the rest of their working lives. This fact tended to make them rather staid and habitual in their work. Historically these men had always been on the Somerset & Dorset, never on the Midland, so following the 1923 amalgamation they carried on as before.

The S&D had always been run in a free and easy style, with no one being worried over something so trivial as losing two minutes, whereas on the Midland things were very different. If you lost two minutes with a Bath to Gloucester express or even a fast goods, your superiors would want to know the reason why. On the Dorset a crew would arrive at Evercreech Junction, and while the engine was unhooked at the Upper Yard, then taken to the table and turned, the shunter marshalled a train for them to take back. The crew might have a meal and stay for an hour or perhaps two, and then eventually the yard foreman would green light them back, they would couple up and set off. Nobody bothered to look at a watch to see what time it was because generally it did not matter if they were a few minutes late. This was their method of working – so consequently the old Dorset drivers and most of their firemen had a dread of the Midland Railway.

Many passed firemen learned on the Dorset road and some Midland men came to work at Bath, men like Stan Bonfield, Ern Buckridge and George Allcock, to whom the Midland way was standard practice. To them the Dorset was like going on a scenic railway out in the country – they had no objection to working on the S&D, it was like a holiday for them, but they simply could not understand the attitude of mind of the Dorset men. But that attitude was there and it was ingrained in young firemen and passed firemen alike. When passed for driving they signed for Bournemouth and might, if pressed, sign for Westerleigh and Avonmouth, but certainly they would not sign to go on the Midland to Gloucester or Birmingham – that was a foreign country as far as they were concerned. This somewhat parochial outlook was advantageous for Bob and a few others who had experience of the North Western and Midland. It was easy to travel from Bath to Birmingham and back once the road had been learned thoroughly and Bob much preferred travelling to the Midlands than to Bournemouth.

Bob fired for Sammy Randall in the Dorset passenger link which had six turns. One was working pilot to the Mail, the 2.20am from Bath to Evercreech Junction, where they came off and turned the engine before working a train tender-first to Templecombe, it being standard practice not to turn there. They then worked the first train to Bath, stopping at all stations, leaving at 7.15am and arriving in Bath at 8.58am. The five coaches were usually worked by Class 2P 4–4–0 Nos 696, 697, 698, 699 or 700.

Bob said that when he was taking a Down train over the S&D he built up the fire as the engine backed on to the train, three or four minutes before the 'right away' time. It was routine procedure to take the dart and prise up the fire in three places, on the right, on the left then in the centre, giving it room to swell. The firehole door would then be closed, leaving the smokebox jet slightly on to keep the fire pulling a little. If the boiler was satisfactory – that is, with the glass almost full of water – then he felt prepared.

Class 2P 4–4–0 No. 40696 at the southern end of Combe Down Tunnel with a Bath to Templecombe train.
(26.4.52 R.E. Toop)

Class 2P 4–4–0 No. 698 near Standish Junction with a Down express.
(c. 1936 Author's collection)

Bob looked back at the guard. When he gave the 'right away' signal, Bob checked that the starter signal was off and said to his driver 'Right away'. It was the fireman's duty, not the driver's, to watch the train safely out of the station, for the driver was supposed to be looking forward. During the first few hundred yards steam pressure fell 5–6lb from full. In that distance the fire was made incandescent by the exhaust up the blast pipe drawing more air through the grate, and generally, steam pressure would return to the mark without Bob having to pick up his shovel. This meant that the engine was ready to release steam via the safety valves and Bob did not want that to happen because it was very wasteful of coal and water. Blowing off could throw as much as 20 gallons of water a minute into the air and that meant that he had shovelled the coal to heat that water to no purpose. So, immediately Bob spotted that the gauge was back on the mark, he turned the injector on, which knocked the boiler pressure back 5lb. Then he closed the injector and commenced firing for the first time, the engine now being at Bath Junction, half a mile from the station.

Using his shovel he glanced at the fire to see which part of the box most needed firing – whether it was thin at the front or too heavy at the back. Although the condition of the rear of the fire was usually visible, he could not see the front without using his shovel as a reflector or deflector. The trick was to use the back of the shovel as a mirror – the flame reflecting on the shovel as he moved it around in a semi-circle. Turning the blade over would deflect incoming air and take the flame off the top of the fire just momentarily while he took a fleeting glance.

Bob Ford found that the water at Highbridge was sometimes contaminated with salt from sea water, so when any of the Bath engines travelled to the town there was always a risk that they would return with a tank of polluted water. When it reached the boiler it caused foaming, with the danger of subsequent priming. The presence of the salt meant that Highbridge engines ideally required a boiler washout every 6 to 10 days instead of the 12 to 16 days of those at Bath. About the ninth day after a boiler washout a Highbridge driver would complain about his engine priming; he would repeat the complaint vociferously on the tenth day and refuse to take it out on the eleventh. They had good reason: there was nothing worse than a locomotive priming. If an engine was doing it you were beaten from the start because, even if she had a full head of steam, you could not ask her for effort because immediately you did, as soon as the regulator was opened, the water rose up and was carried up the main steam pipe into the steam chest and straight into the cylinders. It would then be forced out of the exhaust and up the chimney. The water could be seen emerging: black smoke suddenly went white; there would be a 'whoosh, whoosh, whoosh'; lubrication was washed away and the fire pulled to pieces. Priming upset the equilibrium of everything. The driver had to shut down, then pick her up gently while the fireman had to start mending the fire.

A boiler washout was quite an undertaking, needing about four days. When an engine came in the shed it was left standing for 24 hours with no fire so it grew cool enough to remove the doors from the mud holes. Plugs in the washout holes on the firebox shell were then removed, as were the mud hole doors all along the boiler panels, and then water was injected at high pressure, perhaps as much as 200lb psi, using a stout hosepipe fitted with a nozzle. This detached the scale, of which as much as a barrowful of pieces

Bath's water softener can be seen behind Class 8F 2–8–0 No. 48444. '82F' is chalked on the smokebox and '82F Bath Green Park' on the tender.

(*c.* 1963 R.J. Cannon/Author's collection)

might be collected. The task completed, the mud hole doors were made secure and plugs replaced in the washout holes, except for one on the footplate about level with the gauge glass, this being used for refilling the boiler. When half an inch of water showed in the gauge glass, the water was turned off and the hole sealed with a plug.

The water at Bath was hard, so a water softening plant was installed in the 1930s when the LMS authorities discovered that if the water supply over the whole system could be brought to a purity of that found naturally in Scotland, £1m could be saved annually in boiler maintenance costs. The company's 5,500 locomotives were also fitted with continuous blowdown valves so that a small quantity of water was continually drained from the boiler when the regulator was open, this having the effect of keeping down the surface scum formed by the chemical action of the softened water (where water softening was in use) and therefore helping to prevent priming. Although the quantity of water lost via the blowdown valve was small (1–1½ gallons every minute), an engineman whose locomotive was shy on steam would unscrew the nut at the top, remove the blowdown valve and insert a farthing or sixpence before replacing the valve and locking it again. This modification prevented the valve exuding any water from the boiler.

After this practice had gone on for some time, the LMS headquarters at Derby issued an edict that in future such conduct would be severely dealt with, because blowdowns were added for benefit and purpose and must be allowed to do their work irrespective of whether the crew was struggling for steam or not. In fact, the blowdown did not use much steam, and compared with a boiler's output per hour the proportion used by the blowdown valve was not really worth considering, but drivers looked for every means to save steam. Moreover, if they felt they had had an easier trip because of what they had done, then it became their regular practice.

When a steam raiser knew it was time to light an engine up, in other words about 8 hours before she was wanted for traffic, he threw about 7–8cwt of coal into the firebox, leaving a space in the centre under the firehole door. Then he added half a dozen firelighters with another dozen coal lumps on top, left the damper open, closed the firebox door and left her to her own devices. Black smoke poured out of the cracks round the door and blackened everything in the cab so that one could always tell by its appearance when an engine had been lit up. It could take four hours before she started to generate steam. The steam raiser would occasionally return and add a few more lumps to the fire. He was not concerned about making a lot of steam: as long as he raised 40–50lb before the engine was due out for traffic, then he had done his job and the rest was the responsibility of the crew. Bob had to remember to test the injectors before he had built the fire up to any great extent because if they failed to work he was the one who had to throw the fire out again.

The half-inch of water in the glass was now on the move, merrily bubbling up and down. As pressure rose from zero up to 10lb of steam, the water went up half an inch and by the time 40lb was reached one-third of the glass was full owing to the expansion of the hot water. The boiler also expanded on its channel and moved ⅞ths of an inch towards the cab.

When firing an engine from Bath to Gloucester, the last thing Bob did before leaving the shed was coaling and filling the tender with water; only then did the engine leave the depot and back on to the train. Bob now let her have a full head of steam because the fire was ready for the journey and the boiler was right, having used about 150 gallons of water since leaving the shed to bring the water to the level he desired for the start. The amount of coal and water used depended on the weight of the train and how the engine was worked. For example, with ten coaches weighing a total of 350–400 tons, an average 'Jubilee' or 'Black Five' would have used 2,500 gallons of water, at the rate of something like 50 gallons a minute, and would have burnt a minimum of 56lb of coal per mile, the exact amount depending on the condition of the engine, by the time she reached Gloucester, a distance of 42 miles.

When an engine was working, the exhaust injector was used to put water into the boiler, to save live steam. A 2in-diameter pipe led to the delivery clack from the injector which contained a combining cone below the point where water met steam, the partial vacuum created driving it to the delivery cone to lift the clack against boiler pressure with the momentum acquired. The clack was a one-way valve with the boiler pressure on one side and impetus plus pressure on the other side to admit water to the boiler. No matter what the weather, no matter how cold, Bob never knew an injector to freeze, not even on the LNWR engines which had an old-fashioned system where he had to move a lever to open the tender feed to allow water to gravitate from the tender to the combining cone of the injector. When he was at Ryecroft shed he occasionally

Class 5 2–6–0 No. 42900 at Westerleigh Yard.
(August 1964 W.F. Grainger)

experienced trouble with the LNWR 'Super D' 0–8–0s when coal which had accidentally fallen through the filler hole for replenishing the tank gradually formed silt in the bottom and blocked the exit pipe. The cure for this was to open the steam valve to blow back into the tender and force it clear.

LNWR injectors were tricky because there was no visible sign that they were working; unlike some engines the overflow was not outside but underneath the cab, so if Bob could not hear the injector, the only way he could tell if it was working was to place his hand on the clack box. If it was not being cooled by fresh water, he knew the injector was not functioning. With the exhaust injector he could look over the cab side and see visually. Some engines were wasteful of water because they had an overflow even when they were working properly, but a good injector picked up the water every time.

The Davies & Metcalfe injector had about seven cones and a shuttle valve to switch from live steam to exhaust steam or vice versa as the driver opened or shut the regulator, but it was subject to much wear and was therefore not always a blessing. A good exhaust injector was certainly a boon, but Bob believed nine out of ten were not as good as they should have been and consequently wasted more steam than they were worth. He said that quite a number of firemen would step over to the driver's side of the cab and turn the live steam injector on rather than fiddle with the exhaust injector. Nevertheless Bob declared that when an exhaust injector was functioning properly, its saving was immense because it worked on steam that would otherwise have exhausted uselessly up the chimney.

Live steam injectors were sometimes difficult to start, especially if the clack box was sticky, which caused the steam to blow back. Bob said that you could not shut the steam off without getting a spanner and screwing in the square-ended plug that returned the clack to its seating. The problem could be caused by a small piece of limescale no bigger than a penny getting between the clack and its seating, allowing steam from the boiler to escape straight out.

Bob had experience of this after he had become a driver. One night he was taking a Birmingham goods train out of Bath, with a good fireman called Bernard West. They had not reached Avondale Road, just beyond Weston station, before the 'Crab's' injector blew out twice. The clack was sticking and so Bernard used a spanner to screw in the plug. Bob suggested that he use the live steam injector from then on because the slightest oscillation caused his own to blow out.

They left Bath with a light train of approximately seventeen wagons. On arrival at Westerleigh marshalling yard, where they called to collect more wagons, Bob climbed down from the footplate to speak to the yard inspector, asking how many wagons they were adding on. 'Fifty-eight,' came the reply. Bob exlaimed, 'You aren't! I'll phone Control. I've a wonky exhaust feed injector and I can only rely on the live steam and if that lets me down I'm done altogether, so I'm not taking a full load.' Bob duly spoke to Control and advised them of the position, continuing, 'I advise you that if this engine is going beyond Gloucester [Bob only had to drive it as far as there], that you replace it, letting the Gloucester men bring their own engine off shed and I'll take mine to Gloucester depot. If this engine isn't changed, the crew could be in severe trouble because you shouldn't go on a main line with only one injector.' Had Bob reported the fault before leaving Bath shed it would either have been corrected or he would have been given another engine, but when he inspected the 'Crab' before departure it was perfect – the fault only developed once she was on the move and rocking. Faults did not always show until an engine was out on the road.

Chapter Three

BILL BAGNALL TRANSFERS TO BRISTOL

In 1926 Bill Bagnall moved from Aston to Bristol as a registered fireman with wages of £2 17s per 48 hour week. He was about a dozen firing turns short of 313, the figure that brought with it a further 6s a week for the next two years' firing. After that, the rate was increased to £3 6s until 10 years' firing had been completed when it reached £3 12s, the rate for first-year drivers.

One day in the early 1930s Bill was cleaning the fire of Class 2P 4–4–0 No. 697 in the Down side lay-by at Gloucester. It had worked the 9.15am stopping passenger from Bristol to Gloucester and he and Driver Jim Davies were returning with the 'Pines Express' on its Gloucester to Bath leg. The overall timing was easy, but point-to-point timing was a different matter. Although the distance of 31½ miles from Gloucester to Mangotsfield North Junction was allowed 31 minutes, the first 7 miles included a climb of 1½ miles at a gradient of 1 in 104, and took 10 minutes working the engine to its limit. If only one more minute was used here, that only allowed 20 minutes to cover the remaining 24½ miles – and that with a rising gradient of 5 miles at 1 in 281 between the independent block at Wick (between Berkeley Road and Charfield) and Yate limekiln.

No. 697 had special piston valves with double exhaust channels allowing a rapid release of steam, but this did not assist the speeding so essential from Standish Junction to Wickwar. Her steaming propensity was marred by the fact that she had old LNWR firebars, with their ends flattened to enable them to rest on MR bar racks. Had they been MR bars with shoulders at top, centre and bottom to maintain a reasonable air space, things would have been fine, but the LNWR bars left hardly any air space in the MR rack. (LNWR firebar carriers were designed to hold the firebars apart and aid combustion of even mediocre types of coal.) Removing a bar or two from this makeshift arrangement would have assisted combustion, but this trick could not be resorted to otherwise the complete set of bars would have fallen into the ash pan.

In order to achieve maximum combustion, Bill cleaned the fire of very thin but nevertheless solid clinker. With limestone spread on the bars to keep some air space, he knew that he would at least have as good a start as possible. Had he left the clinker *in situ* it would soon have sealed the small apertures between the bars and prevented free steaming just where they needed it most.

While he was shovelling out the clinker, a Down express ran in. After its departure it left on the platform Chief Locomotive Inspector Follows, who watched Bill's efforts on No. 697, eventually calling him over to explain what he was doing. Bill told him about the firebars. Follows queried, 'And what do you know about LNWR firebars?' Bill replied, 'I've dropped many a thousand as a bar boy at Aston Loco.' Follows then asked

The sister engine to No. 697, this is Class 2P 4–4–0 No. 40696 of 71G (Bath) in BR lined livery at its home shed.
(*c.* 1952 Colin Roberts)

Bill to pick up a small piece of clinker and wrap it in paper so that he could put it in his case.

Almost forgetting the incident, Bill returned to his engine. Meanwhile, on the Up platform Follows spoke to Local Footplate Inspector George Arkwright who was seeing him off back to Derby. Arkwright then came running over to the Down platform as No. 697 was reversing on to the 'Pines Express'. He called, 'Why didn't you tell me about the LNWR bars and the trouble they're causing on that engine?' Just then the guard waved his flag and with a toot on the whistle they left. Driver Jim Davies commented, 'What's the matter with him? He's put out about something.' The result was that Follows had No. 697 and a sister engine recalled to Derby for their firebars to be changed.

Bill encountered Arkwright again following the Charfield accident. On 13 October 1928 Class 3 4–4–0 No. 714, heading the Leeds to Bristol mail, ran through signals and

Wickwar seen from the cab of a locomotive heading an Up train.
(1963 W.F. Grainger)

hit a goods train being reversed by GWR 2–6–0 No. 6381 into a refuge siding. Unfortunately, No. 714 was derailed into the path of an Up goods train. The wooden-bodied coaches were gas-lit and ignited in a terrible blaze lasting for 12 hours. Bill was firing to Driver Bob Davies on the engine attached to the Saltley crane, which assisted in clearing the wreckage. They needed to run to Sharpness to get water. Travelling on the footplate with them was George Arkwright, then acting as 'Station' – a man appointed following an accident to act as a local control over the length between the crash site and Berkeley Road South Junction signal box.

Bill had another experience with a Class 2P 4–4–0. He was working the Down Night Mail and as they passed through Yate his driver said, 'Run the boiler down a bit so that I can give her a bit extra through to Westerleigh'. They passed Yate at around 60mph with the water now at the bottom nut. As Mangotsfield North distant signal was clear, the driver cut off steam and Bill turned on the injector to get some water into the gauge glass.

Normally Bill's mate would have braked to go round the curve through Mangotsfield station, but that night he took a risk. By the time they reached Mangotsfield North

View of the wreckage below the bridge at Charfield. GWR 2–6–0 No. 6381 can be seen in front of the
steam crane.
(13.10.28 Author's collection)

Class 3F 0–6–0 No. 43507 with a Down freight passing under the bridge where the 1928 disaster occurred.
(11.5.61 Author)

The view from the cab of a Down locomotive approaching Charfield. The coal train, left, stands in the siding into which the GWR train was setting back in 1928. The shiny top of the driver's cap can be seen in the bottom right corner.
(1963 W.F. Grainger)

Class 3F 0–6–0 No. 43507 taking water at Charfield.
(11.5.61 Author)

Junction their speed had been reduced to about 40mph and they experienced a rough ride through the station, but the junction beyond caused no problems. On they coasted through the cutting and Staple Hill Tunnel, and at Fishponds they were about a minute and a half down on time, but Bill's driver said that could be accounted for running into Bristol Temple Meads. They gained speed down the 1 in 69 bank. Had the driver run the engine hard and had to brake round Mangotsfield curve, steam would have been required to power the engine from Mangotsfield North Junction to Fishponds, and with low steam pressure they could have experienced difficulty blowing the vacuum brake off. What impressed Bill was the driver running about 6 miles to Bristol without using any steam beyond Shortwood Sidings signal-box.

Driver Walter Baldwin, nicknamed 'Snatcher', was another exponent of the skill of train coasting. One night when working the 1.10am Bristol to Birmingham mail, it was foggy and the platelayers had been called out to place warning detonators at signals. On the quadruple track section, as they approached Bromsgrove South Junction distant signal at about 50mph, a detonator exploded, so Snatcher closed the regulator, allowed the train to slow down and applied the brake. Drawing to a standstill in the dense fog Snatcher told Bill to go and check the signal. Bill climbed down from the footplate. He was unable to see the signal in the dense fog but knew how to find it. First, he placed his hand on the relief line to check if any train was moving on it, then he stepped over and groped for the signal wires at the lineside. The wires were supported on small stakes, a series of which ran from Bromsgrove South box. Bill knew that the number of wires he could feel in the foggy darkness would tell him if they had passed the outer home. Four wires meant they had passed the signals, but if he felt only the two wires for the distant signals that would indicate that they had yet to reach the outer home signals. Bill walked beside the wires for about twenty paces before reaching the signal gantry. One weight was in the up position, indicating that one of the signals above was off. Visibility was too poor to see whether it was the relief or main line signal that showed clear, so Bill had to climb the ladder to make sure it was the Up main which was off. It was, so he returned to the footplate to report his finding to Snatcher.

Snatcher also imparted to Bill nuggets of signal information. For instance, as an ex-Burton man, he knew that when approaching the town from Derby South, if the Wetmore Junction distant signal was off this meant that you had a clear road into Burton station; likewise the distant signal at Tramway Junction, Gloucester, took you right through the station for a run up the bank beyond. Cudworth South distant locked you right through the four Cudworth boxes. He also told Bill that Saltley station distant on the Washwood Heath gantry took you to Proof House Junction and the three-aspect signal there allowed trains right into the platform, but light engines could be held at the No. 3 signal.

'Snatcher' acquired his nickname from his manner of braking, as he held firmly to the principle that 'You never break a train [coupling] by putting the brake on, but you can easily break a train when you attempt to get it off.' The soundness of Snatcher's braking technique was illustrated to Bill one night when they were working the 9.18pm Mail from Birmingham New Street, calling at Barnt Green, Blackwall, Bromsgrove, Stoke Works, Droitwich and Worcester on its run to Bristol. At Bromsgrove they were turned into the

The sharp curve at Mangotsfield, looking Up.
(*c.* 1960 Lens of Sutton)

platform road and as they regained the main line at Bromsgrove South Bill heard a clanging sound, as if a clinker shovel had fallen from the back of the tender. Bill took the precaution of looking back to see if he could spot anything, but noticed nothing out of the ordinary. He knew his fire irons were secure because he had checked them at New Street. In due course the train called at Stoke Works, Droitwich and then Worcester, where they eased up to the water crane. While Bill filled the tender, a wheel-tapper went round checking the train. Returning to Bill, he said, 'Come and have a look back here, Bristol'. Bill went.

Between the second and third parcel vans he noticed a space of at least a foot, with the vacuum and heating pipes stretched almost to their limit. The tapper got down on the permanent way and said, 'The spring under the floor used for coupling the hook and buffers has broken and part of it is missing. The drawgear is only held by the four face-plate bolts on the main bogie frame!' Bill thought to himself, 'Ah, and I know where that missing bit is — somewhere near Bromsgrove South box', but he kept his own counsel on the matter. Fortunately there was not much traffic to transfer to the next van, as the damaged one had to be removed by the station pilot while Bill's engine stood in the bay platform.

A Class 5 4–6–0 at Blackwell, with an Up Fyffe's banana train. The vehicles are Vanfits.
(*c.* 1964 Richard Brown)

Bromsgrove, looking north. The Lickey Incline begins beyond the bridge. The centre road is the through
Down line.
(*c.* 1960 Lens of Sutton)

Bill realised that Snatcher's theory of braking had indisputable benefits: had the brake been released before stopping, the weight of the train could easily have broken the train into two. Even so, his method of braking tested the nerves of some firemen and some never relished working with him. Bill believed that many were secretly of the opinion that 'Old Baggy' had been with Snatcher for so long he was case-hardened to his method and took no notice.

The highest accolade a driver can give his fireman is to trust him to drive, or allow anyone to take the driver's place 'providing that his fireman is on the footplate'. Snatcher certainly trusted Bill after over three years of express work together. One Monday Bill and Snatcher ran their Class 4P 4–4–0 Compound light engine from Barrow Road to Temple Meads to take over the Up 'Devonian' and, as usual, the strings under the train had to be pulled to unseat the brake cylinder ball valves and so equalise the vacuum above and below the brake pistons because the Western ran on 25in of vacuum and the Midland on 21in. When they reversed their engine on to the train, which always had a brake compo at each end, a couple of enginemen approached Bill and said, 'We're two drivers road-learning. Do you think your mate will allow the two of us to ride the footplate?' Bill replied that he knew for certain Snatcher would not permit four men to ride on an express engine, so the two Derby men decided between themselves who would ride on the footplate and who would travel in the brake compartment.

Only 42 minutes was allowed for the 37 miles to Gloucester and with a load of 290 tons this was hard going in view of the 3-mile climb out of Bristol, much of it at 1 in 69. Yate, 10¼ miles from the start, needed to be passed as much under 20 minutes as possible, leaving 22 minutes for the remaining 27 miles to Gloucester. Bill said that Compounds could do 80mph with ease on the level, or near level, and from Yate to Berkeley Road 90mph was possible.

Exactly 42 minutes after leaving Temple Meads they stopped at Gloucester for water. The Derby man travelling in the van emerged and asked Bill, 'How about if I do the firing and you ride in the van?' Bill agreed. He climbed down from the tender and entered the brake compartment to take it easy on the guard's seat and look forward through the small window in the ducket.

The 16 minutes allowed for the 19¼ miles from Ashchurch to Dunhampstead was a tight timing. As they passed through Defford, through his window Bill saw the long pricker or rake being swung round – which meant that whoever was doing the firing was finding it hard to maintain the 200lb psi pressure. Bill had a quiet grin to himself.

Eventually they ran into New Street. Bill left the van and saw the two Derby men leave the engine. As he passed, one said 'You earn your money firing to that old so-and-so.' Bill climbed on the footplate to be greeted by Snatcher saying, 'Thee's better have a look at the fire, they've both been messing with it.' In Snatcher's opinion those two Derby men were no match for Bill. He looked into the firebox and decided that there was too much coal under the arch, so to correct this he set the damper to work on that part of the grate and by the time they reached the water troughs at Haselour, north of Tamworth, matters were restored.

Bill fired to Snatcher for over three years, from 1932 to 1935, in Express Link No. 1, the Leeds section. The link originally comprised four sets of men, but when Barrow

Class 4P Compound No. 1000 hauling a semi-fast train near Mangotsfield.
(6.4.36 S. Miles Davey)

Class 4P 4–4–0 Compound No. 1059 near Mangotsfield with the 10.35am Bristol to Sheffield, with through coaches to Newcastle and Edinburgh.
(6.4.36 S. Miles Davey)

Ashchurch, looking Down, with the level crossing signal-box (closed 27.7.58) on the left.
(*c.* 1954 Dr A.J.G. Dickens/Author's collection)

Road Depot was allocated some Sheffield trips the link was increased to six sets. There were another six sets in the Derby section. Drivers getting on in years did not take kindly to too much lodging work and really hated the private lodging necessary after booking off at Millhouses Depot, Sheffield.

As Snatcher approached retirement, Jimmy Davies, the man who was to take his place in the link, spent a month learning the road from Derby to Leeds. In the third week he was to travel on the footplate of the 'Devonian'. Snatcher got off the engine and greeted him with the words 'Hello Titch'. Davies was so nicknamed because he was the smallest of the three Davies at the depot. It spoke volumes for Snatcher's status that he was able to address him as Titch, for it was a name Bill would never have used to his face. Snatcher continued, 'Bist thee going to have my job?' 'Yes Walter, when I've signed for the road.' 'Well,' said Walter, 'this is one of the jobs you'll be working, why not try it out?' Jimmy stepped aboard with his box. Snatcher opened the basket compartment at the front of the tender, grabbed his own black leather engineman's holdall, and then got off the engine and entered the brake compartment at the front of the train.

Jimmy coped well with the tight timing, but soon after leaving New Street, while running through Saltley station, he felt a jerk as the brakes were touched. Snatcher, in the brake compartment, had used the guard's brake valve to ease speed over the railway tunnel used by the Birmingham gas company, whose works at that point were on both sides of the line. A permanent 30mph restriction was in force there and Snatcher himself had been carpeted for exceeding it on a couple of occasions, hence his brief brake application from the van. Titch was surprised to be told by Bill that Snatcher was shaking his fist through the guard's window. He said gloomily, 'I suppose Walter will come up to the footplate now.' Bill replied, 'If Snatcher comes on the footplate, it will be to do the driving.' Jimmy was quiet and kept asking Bill to look out for the signals. Bill quickly reassured him that not only did he observe all the signals, but that Snatcher in the van would not miss one either.

When they arrived at Sheffield Jimmy was really sweating with the effort, but Bill was certain that this trip had made him into an express man much quicker than a month's riding behind other men would have done. Bill was his mate for about 15 months until Bill himself passed for driving.

One cold, wintry evening Bill and Titch were working the 4.48pm Derby to Bristol, which ran straight through Burton to New Street. The carriage heaters required a pressure of 30lb psi from the engine to work efficiently. As the train entered New Street South Tunnel, a flexible connection, or 'bag', of the heating pipe between two of the coaches burst and in the tunnel it sounded just as though the train had exploded a detonator.

Jimmy immediately slammed on the brake and the train was almost stationary when Bill rushed over to calm him down and opened the large ejector in an attempt to blow the brakes off. But it was too late and the engine came to a halt with its chimney just outside the tunnel. Jimmy made a couple of attempts to start the train, but the engine soon slipped to a standstill on the steep gradient.

Bill had noticed that the carriage warming gauge had fallen to zero and shouted 'Bag's gone' when he took action to try to release the brakes. The standard procedure in the event of a flexible pipe breaking was to wire forward for 'a fitter and renewal', but there they were stuck in the south tunnel apparently needing an assisting engine.

Bill walked forward to New Street No. 3 signal-box where he saw the chief inspector standing by the door. A short siding known as 'The Parlour' held a Deeley 0–6–4T and its driver, seeing Bill going to the box, asked, 'Got yer wrong line order?' and Bill had to admit that in the excitement he had overlooked the necessary form to enable the assisting engine to enter the already occupied section. 'Here kid,' said the driver, 'I always keep one in my waistcoat pocket,' and he gave Bill the essential piece of paper. Bill arrived at the foot of the flight of stairs leading to the signal-box to be greeted by the chief inspector asking, 'Have you got your Wrong Line Order?' 'Yes,' was the reply, 'but it ain't made out.' The chief inspector responded with, 'Come up here and make it out and I'll arrange for an assisting engine.'

While this was going on, Titch had been busy. He was down on the ground taking sand from the locomotive's sandboxes and coating the rails with it. After sanding the length he estimated was sufficient, he climbed back on the footplate with the idea of trying to release the brake and move forward into the station.

Deeley 0–6–4T No. 2029 at Saltley.
(9.5.36 Colin Roberts collection)

While Bill was filling out the form on the signalman's desk, the chief inspector walked to the assisting engine and rode back on her to the signal-box. Having completed his clerical work, Bill also mounted the footplate of this engine, crewed by Bath men, who were to couple on in front to get Bill's engine home.

Just then Titch opened the regulator to give two puffs and then opened it fully, almost blowing off the corner of the tunnel. The chief inspector was furious. 'Doesn't your mate known that having issued a Wrong Line Order he MUST NOT move his train?' They backed the assistant engine on to Titch's engine, the Bath fireman hooking on while the irate chief inspector furiously rebuked Titch for attempting to move his train.

There was Titch, on his perch in a filthy state after his attempts at sanding, his tie out of the rubber collar he favoured and his mind in a turmoil over the whole incident. Bill subtly pulled at his overall coat, trying to put him wise, but Titch was too distracted and so Bill kept silent, hoping that in the haste to move the train, which was blocking a busy line, matters would be overlooked.

Titch got on his high horse when Bill eventually told him about obtaining a Wrong Line Order from the shunting engine driver, but he was soon put in his place when Bill told him that it was the driver who should have supplied one, and it should already have been made out.

LMS Wrong Line Order: Driver to Signalman.

The result was that Bill agreed to make out a report to cover the incident. It read: 'Whilst approaching New Street, observed the Distant signal "on". Stopped to ascertain the position of the Home signal. Could not re-start the train owing to slippery rail. Carried out the conditions of Rule 183(g) to arrive at the station.'

When he read this at Bristol Titch nearly hit the roof of the enginemen's lobby. 'What about the bang and the fact that the distant is always "on"?' he demanded. 'Ah,' Bill replied, 'but only we know that. The chief clerk don't, and who's going to tell him? The only time you'll get a green light on that "peg" is when you're on a through goods train when you wait there on a red 'un until the bobby in No. 5 has got you the road through to Church Road Junction. Then it'll quickly switch from red to amber and green because they don't want a goods train stopping in New Street station.'

After Bill had fully explained this piece of enginemen's lore, Titch was more amenable to the action proposed and entered the report. Both men were greatly relieved when no repercussions followed.

On another occasion Bill and Jimmy were on the 6.45am lodging turn and after a rest at Siddals Road, Derby, they booked on to work an express known as the 'Scotsman' because a couple of the carriages came through from Edinburgh. While preparing their 'Black Five', a steam raiser passing by asked, 'Who's your contact with the top brass?' Bill failed to see the point of the question, until the man explained that their tender was full of the best Frickley coal. Bill's previous experience of this coal was when he had worked the Duke of Beaufort's special train from Temple Meads to Aintree – twelve first-class coaches accompanied by two kitchen cars to supply the passengers' needs from 7.00am until midnight. Both the engines of this special double-headed train had had Frickley coal and he vividly remembered that on their return to Bristol his engine could have done the whole journey again with merely a shaking of the bars. It was beautiful coal – a real fireman's delight.

With their 'Black Five' they set off from Derby shed to the station, there to await the arrival of their train. Bill's only criticism of the coal was that it was all in huge lumps which needed to be broken up to pass through the firehole door. Before reaching New Street Bill realised that all he needed to do was 'chuck it in and work the dampers' – steam was there for the asking.

At New Street they had a 40 minute wait for other connecting trains. While Titch made the tea, Bill decided to fill the firebox, starting at the front under the brick arch and working back until he had filled the box right up. They left New Street a little earlier than Bill had anticipated, but he closed the firehole doors and opened the front and back dampers. He experienced a few anxious moments before reaching Bournville,

Bromsgrove, looking Up.
(16.4.53 Dr A.J.G. Dickens/Author's collection)

Class 2P 4–4–0 No. 518 and Class 4P Compound No. 1057 near Abbot's Wood Junction with the 10.35am ex-Bristol, Temple Meads.
(*c.* 1933 Colin Roberts collection)

Bredon, looking Up.
(*c.* 1910 Author's collection)

thinking that he might have choked the fire, but from there onwards he knew he had a winner. Bromsgrove station was passed, then Dunhampstead and Abbot's Wood Junction where the line via Worcester joined. Bill noticed that Titch was looking at him rather keenly. Bill glanced in the box at Bredon, 36 miles from New Street. Then they noticed the adverse Ashchurch distant signal. As they rolled up to the home signal it was pulled off and Bill put on some more coal. Titch commented, 'Do you know you ain't opened them doors since New Street?' Bill said, 'Yes, I know, and if it hadn't been for them pegs being on at Ashchurch, we'd have gone from Brum [Birmingham] to Cheltenham on one firebox full of Frickley.'

Sometimes Bill was able to spot management errors. On the MR there was a system for signalling before a junction, whereby the two signals would be so positioned that the one used for passenger trains was higher than the one for goods. Following the formation of the LMS in 1923, the position of the signals was altered so that a speed restriction would determine which signal was the highest. Footplatemen at Barrow Road enjoyed a fine lecture on this new principle by Mr Saddler of the signalling department. When Bill saw new signals being erected at Stoke Works Junction, where there was a restriction of 60mph towards Spetchley and 30mph towards Droitwich, he was astounded to see the signals exactly as they had been before, with the higher signal for the Droitwich line. Bill wrote to Chief Inspector Bashford at Derby, who was in charge of the Locomen's Improvement Class matters, asking if Mr Saddler's information had been altered.

Returning from Leeds to Bristol, it was standard practice to stop well back on Derby No. 4 platform to uncouple the locomotive, then draw forward to take water while a shunting engine added a coach and dining car to the seven-coach train. One day when they stopped, there was Mr Bashford, together with a colleague and a fireman. The fireman was instructed to take Bill's place and carry out station duties while the men talked. The conversation went like this:

Bashford: 'You are Fireman Bagnall, secretary of the Barrow Road Improvement Class?'
Bagnall: 'Yes.'
Bashford: 'You reported some signals at Stoke Works Junction?'
Bagnall: 'Well, I don't know about reporting signals, but I did inquire if the lecture given by Mr Saddler was authentic in view of what was erected there.'

Bashford then produced two rough sketches of the four Down signals at Stoke Works Junction, *viz*:

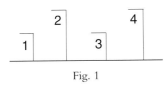

Fig. 1

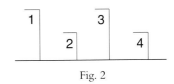

Fig. 2

1. Relief to Spetchley
2. Relief to Droitwich
3. Main to Spetchley
4. Main to Droitwich

He showed Bill Fig. 1. The conversation continued:

Bashford: 'Are the new signals erected like this?'
Bagnall: 'No.'
Bashford: 'Are they like this?' (He then showed Bill Fig. 2.)
Bagnall: 'Yes.'

Within a week the signals were changed in line with the speed restrictions and as Saddler had informed them.

Bill fired on expresses for over four years. When he was paired with Driver Bill Janes, he hardly said a word during the first week. At the end of that week Janes gave him some advice. 'Bill, you work far too hard; it ain't as hard as you've made it this week. Just remember that I, too, have done my firing and I recognise that you want the steam gauge to be just below the red mark, and the water level to show half a glass, but don't try to be a perfectionist. Just do as you do on a goods train: prepare for the hard bits and your driver, if he's any good, will accept the ups and downs of steam and water as a natural sequence of doing the job.' The two Bills were great friends after that and Janes taught Bagnall quite a lot about keeping his head when circumstances tried to make him lose it.

One day Bill was fireman on Compound No. 1027. She had just been 'shopped' at Derby, that is, stripped down and any worn parts renewed. For at least a fortnight after returning from Derby, such engines ran stiffly before the moving parts bedded down, so most levers required extra muscle power to operate them. In particular, the reversing gear tended to be stiff.

Arriving punctually at Derby at 5.27am they unhooked from the 1.10am Mail from Bristol, ran over the top crossover at the station and via the Way & Works Road to the unsignalled shed road. They ran over a long siding nicknamed 'Dead Man's Lane', passed over a couple of hand-worked points and then Bill got down to hold over the ashpit points. When they were set correctly he called to his driver Frank Kenton, 'All right, come ahead.' To change direction, Frank had to rotate the reversing handle about a dozen turns from backward into forward gear, no doubt cursing its stiffness as he did so. As No. 1027 started to move, Bill heard an engine approaching them, but owing to the fog he could not see it, but he knew it was on their road. He immediately yelled to Frank to set back, but with such a stiff wheel, Frank was unable to do this quickly. Bill could not run to stop the other engine as he dare not let go of the point lever or the Compound would have been thrown off the road. Before Frank was able to reverse, a Class 5P5F 'Crab' 2–6–0, then numbered in the 13XXX series, in Bill's words 'Clouted us a real pile-driver', resulting in the two engines being locked together and off the road.

Bill hurried to the 'Crab's' footplate and found its driver sitting on his seat, somewhat shocked. He asked, 'Where's my mate?' For a dreadful moment, Bill had visions of the other fireman mangled on the small running step that 'Crabs' had on their front buffer beam, because it was a driver's duty when going off shed to send his fireman forward to ensure that he did not meet an engine going on shed. But before Bill could go and investigate, the fireman came running up from the shed saying, 'That's what you get for running about on a morning like this without me.'

Hughes/Fowler 'Crab' 2–6–0 No. 13000. Notice in the background the LMS coal wagons on the raised
siding leading to the coaling stage.
(*c.* 1928 Author's collection)

The two firemen walked down to the foreman's office to report the incident. The
foreman, hearing the story, exclaimed, 'That just about seals off the shed!' – because the
other end of the shed exit road was blocked by another derailment, which was why the
'Crab' was leaving by Dead Man's Lane. The foreman continued, 'All right Bristol
['foreigners' were always addressed by the name of the shed they came from] get your
belongings and off to the barracks and tell your mate to make out a report on the matter.'
Frank's report was short and to the point. 'Whilst coming from Dead Man's Lane road to
the ash pit, run into by 13XXX. Driver Kenton, Bristol.'

A few days after the incident Bill was called to see District Locomotive Inspector
Whitaker, who questioned him about the incident and carefully noted down all that Bill
told him. When Bill told Driver Frank Kenton that he had seen the superintendent,
Kenton was upset that he had not been called on to offer his own account.

Not many days later, Bill was called to the superintendent's office again. This time a
locomotive inspector was present and Bill was asked to repeat his account of the incident.
Once again Frank was not invited to speak and Bill felt there must be some discrepancy
between the reports of the two drivers.

Then came a day when Bill was kept on shed to be interviewed by Chief Inspector Follows of Derby. Bill asked, 'Why is it that you keep having me in and not Driver Kenton?' Follows replied, 'We have a very good reason. There's something not quite right, as the stories of what happened on that foggy morning are at variance and do not give a clear and straightforward account of what happened.'

Bill pondered on this for a moment or two, then said, 'You speak as if you know that someone is lying.' Follows assented, 'Very true, there's no doubt that someone isn't being truthful.' Bill blurted out, 'Well it ain't Driver Kenton because I saw him make the report out and what he wrote is true.'

Follows searched among the papers, held up one and said, 'I have it here. Tell me what it says, will you?' Bill replied, 'Whilst coming from Dead Man's Lane road to the ash pit, run into by 13XXX. Driver Kenton, Bristol.' 'Word perfect,' Follows replied, 'but it doesn't help a bit.' Bill grasped the challenge and continued, 'Well, if you want to know who was to blame, the damage to the two engines will tell the true story.' Follows said, 'What do you mean, "Tell the true story"?'

Bill continued, 'As you're aware, I was holding the points over to turn our engine on to the ash pit road, and I dared not let go of the point lever or I would have thrown 1027 on the dirt. Although I shouted to Frank to "Set back", I knew that he'd have no time to reverse the engine, it being very stiff having just been shopped. I heard, rather than saw, the engine bearing down on us. Our buffer beam was intact, but the 13XXX's left-hand buffer was embedded in the region of our right-hand low pressure cylinder.' Follows thought for a moment, reflected on the geography of Derby shed, then closed his book, gathered his papers and said, 'I'm satisfied now what happened. You and your driver are in the clear.'

Follows then went off at a complete tangent, asking Bill how he liked express firing. This was an ideal opening for Bill to plug a few of his ideas. 'With an engine coaled with Frickley and tubes and tubeplate clean, the job's a doddle – remove those items and your success varies according to how many of those items are grouped to your disadvantage.' Bill thought this was quite a speech and it was acknowledged with the remark: 'Well, one thing, fireman, you have not only learnt your job, but have thought quite a lot about the matters affecting it.' Bill left that office walking on air and quite pleased to have cleared up the matter. Later he learned from Mr Whitaker that the Derby driver had copied Driver Kenton's report word for word, but modified it to read: 'Run into by engine 1027 whilst coming off the table road to go to Dead Man's Lane.'

Chapter Four

DRIVING EXAMINATION

A fter four or five years of firing on expresses, Bill took his driving examination in 1936. On more than one occasion he had crossed swords with the inspector responsible for passing drivers, and owing to this the inspector intended to give Bill a hard time and not allow him to achieve the necessary 65 marks to pass. Bill knew that the inspector had never been a driver himself and this knowledge stood Bill in good stead during the two days of testing – one day at the shed and another out on the road. Another problem facing a potential driver was the old Midland custom that the examining inspector sought the shed foreman's opinion and this could produce a bias for or against.

On the shed day, they started by 'going round the wheel', the examiner asking where the engine would 'take her steam' – in other words, which cylinder port was open to live steam and which port open to exhaust. The four quarters, the four angles and the fore and back gear made thirty-two port openings to be memorised. This knowledge was considered essential to enable a driver to identify a valve or piston defect and thus report correctly.

The next test involved going into the pit below the engine. The first question was: 'You have a broken back gear eccentric. Explain how you would deal with it and how would you make the engine fit to travel on one cylinder?', Bill's answer shook the locomotive inspector. 'I'd remove the broken parts and travel on TWO cylinders with the engine in full forward gear.' This was not the reply the inspector had expected, so he continued, 'What about taking down the side?' Bill asked, 'What for? I've explained what I'd do with the defect you put to me. Do you question the correctness of my remedy?' The inspector was really stumped, as Bill knew he would be, because he had done very little firing and had never been a driver and so had scant knowledge of the field in which he was supposed to be an expert.

He then asked Bill how he would take down the side of the Class 3F 0–6–0 beside them and make it suitable to travel under its own steam on one cylinder. Now quite a sizeable proportion of this class of locomotive had solid small ends like those found on Class 4F 0–6–0s. These small ends were connected to the piston rod by a three-dimensional gudgeon pin secured by a plate bolted on the inside of the slide block which ran through four slide bars. It was tapered, and displaced the strap and cotter pins found on the older types.

When Bill started his explanation by saying that he would removed the split pins securing the ⅞in nuts on the inside slide block, the inspector revealed his limited knowledge because he thought both large and small ends were held on their journals by

Class 3F 0–6–0 No. 43734 of 82G (Templecombe) arriving at Evercreech Junction with a goods train from Highbridge.
(31.8.60 Author)

a strap and cotter arrangement. The locomotive inspector and Bill emerged from under the engine, the former a slightly wiser man. But Bill was too sensible to display any superiority, as he had to receive at least 65 marks out of 105, comprising 10 marks each for the ten items stated in the exam syllabus, plus 5 marks for appearance.

A second confrontation occurred when Bill was asked a question about making trimmings for conveying lubricating oil to the working surfaces. There are three main types of worsted trimmings: plug, tail and pad. A plug trimming is used for rotating and oscillating parts with sufficient motion to splash oil over the end of a tube into which the plug is fixed. This type of trimming is made by wrapping several strands of worsted lengthwise over a piece of twisted wire to form a plug which fits comfortably in the tube. Tail trimmings are used to lubricate parts such as piston rods and axle box guides and are made of the same material as the plug variety, but the strands are sufficiently long to fit into a siphon tube suspended into the oil box in order to siphon the oil from the reservoir to the area needing lubrication. Pad trimmings are used for die blocks, expansion link pins and axle journals, the pads being saturated with oil each time the locomotive is prepared. Subsequently they gently lubricate during the engine's working.

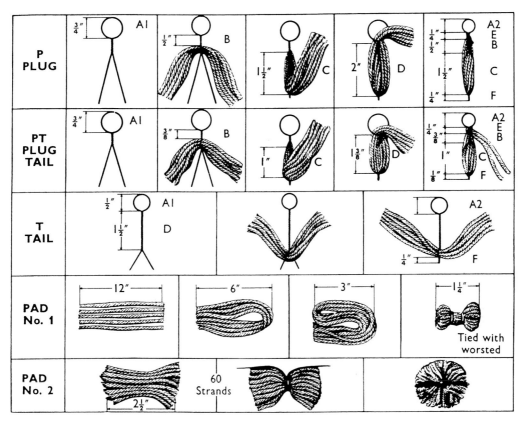

Details of the preparation of worsted trimmings from *A Handbook for Steam Railway Locomotive Firemen*, published by the LMS in 1941.

The 'big end' trimming asked for by the inspector required a large and small cork, a 10in length of trimming wire and eight strands of wool. The finished article had thirty-two strands and was a little over 3in in length. As secretary of the mutual improvement class at the Barrow Road shed, Bristol, Bill had had much practice at making trimmings and was confident of a pass. The test for a trimming was to ensure that the strands would not come apart at the points where the eight strands became thirty-two. However, the inspector unfairly took hold of the trimming, bent it and placed a finger between the fold and with two hands, tugged it apart. 'Try again, will you?' was his request. Bill made another which received the same treatment and was asked to produce a third trimming. This time Bill purposely folded the strands twice across the wire and then offered it to him. Testing the trimming, the inspector was unable to break it and commented, 'Ah, that's better. You'll have to practise a bit on your trimming technique.'

Bill carefully wrapped the two broken trimmings in a piece of paper, deliberately emphasising the action as he knew the inspector would be curious. 'What are you wrapping those up for?' he inquired. 'Well,' he answered, 'if trimmings have to undergo the test that you've made on these two, then the mutual improvement class will have to change its training methods.' The inspector did not know how to reply to that and simply said, 'Let's get on to the rules', picking up the book in order to check Bill's answers. Bill knew the recommendation for this part of the exam and observed, 'I understand that a working knowledge is what is required, rather than reciting rules parrot-fashion. Give me a railway incident and I'll tell you what I'd do in the circumstances.' From then on, the inspector knew that he had met his match and grudgingly passed Bill for driving with a total of 67 marks.

Bob Ford, perhaps owing to wartime conditions, faced a rather less gruelling exam. In April 1944 he was tested for two hours on a shunting engine at Bath, the following day going to a grounded coach body and receiving a four-hour grilling on the rule book. The tests successfully completed, Bob was made a passed fireman.

Bob made his first trip driving as a passed fireman on 6 June 1944. The previous day he had caught the first Down passenger train from Bath at about 7.00am, getting out at Moorewood with Driver Charlie Morris to relieve the men on the stone train. Bob fired it as far as Shepton Mallet where they were themselves relieved and travelled home 'on the cushions'. It was the only easy job in the Dorset link and on that Monday Bob arrived home at about 12.30pm and spent the afternoon and evening with relatives who were staying with him at the time. He anticipated having plenty of time to spend with them during the coming week. After an evening out with them, Bob returned home at about 11.00pm looking forward to a good night's rest. But his mother had waited up to tell him that the call boy had been round. 'Been for me?' he queried. 'Yes, look here's the ticket.' The ticket required him to go on duty at 2.50am for the 4.00am goods, but did not state the destination. Bob said to his mother, 'Couldn't you have told the call boy I was out? The fact that you've accepted this ticket means I've agreed to carry out this turn of duty. If I'd been home, I'd have refused it on the grounds of insufficient rest, but it isn't your fault, mother. I'll go to bed immediately.' So saying he retired to bed and fell asleep at once.

A few hours later the call boy, Smut Woodbury, went in through Bob's front door (which was never locked), climbed silently up the stairs, opened Bob's door and called 'Hello, it's Smut. It's 2.20.' 'All right,' Bob replied. 'I'm out of bed.' Bob always got out of bed immediately because if he did not, he was certain to fall asleep again. Smut, actually a grown man, had been given the job of call boy combined with a post in the stores following a serious operation.

Bob left home at about 2.45am and signed on. Tom Rudd, the night shed foreman told him, 'You've got an Armstrong, Bob. She's on the top shed on the Midland road, just this side of the turntable. Four o'clock goods to Gloucester. There you'll be relieved by Gloucester men. So-and-so's your mate.' Bob had seen this youth about the shed cleaning, but he had not been employed by the railway for long and Bob did not know his name. He was a happy, very willing lad. Bob said to him, 'You know all your duties, don't you? Cleaning and filling those lamps; topping up the sand bins? It's a bit awkward to fill the sand bins up here because the sand furnace is down by the other shed, but we can move the engine along; you can bring a couple of bucketfuls up and I'll tip them in.' Back in the cab Bill said, 'Push your fire over the box, kid, and throw a couple of lumps in with your hands,' and that was what he did.

Ex-Somerset & Dorset 'Armstrong' Class 4F 0–6–0 No. 44558 of 82F (Bath) at its home shed. Notice the coaling stage on the far right.

(*c.* 1961 Dr T.R.N. Edwards)

Bob oiled round and underneath the Class 4F 0–6–0, some examples of which were built by Armstrong, Whitworth & Co., finishing about 10 minutes before they were due off shed. Then he wiped his hands and came to the cab, saying, 'Now I'm just going to the cabin to make a can of tea and when I come back it won't be long before we have to go over to the yard to pick up the wagons.'

A few minutes later Bob returned to the engine, climbed aboard and saw his young fireman putting the shovel away. 'What've you been doing? Cleaning the shovel?' he asked. 'No,' he answered, 'I've been making the fire up.' 'Not with the shovel, I hope.' 'Yes,' he said. Bob looked into the firebox and found it was as black as the ace of spades. He glanced at the damper. 'Thank goodness the damper was open when you made it up.' The engine was a 'foreigner' so he was unaware of her propensity for steaming. Bob 'boxed her up' and put water in the boiler. 'Leave your blower on about an inch and a half and don't touch anything until I tell you. I'll fire and drive. I don't want you to do anything unless I instruct you. Don't do anything I don't tell you. Hasn't anyone ever told you, never, ever put Welsh coal on with a shovel when an engine's standing still?'

'No,' the lad faltered. 'Weren't you taught that on the shunter or on the bank?' 'No, I've never been on the shunter or on the bank.' 'Well, it's not your fault then, kid,' Bob said, 'but what you've done is lethal.' 'Is it?' he asked 'Yes, you'll certainly remember this.'

Bob took the Armstrong off shed and over to the goods yard, running slowly, deliberately delaying backing on to the train for as long as possible. After Bob had coupled up the guard came along and informed them of the load. Bob explained that he had an awkward fire and intended taking his time until he was out on the main line and the engine was right.

Bob slowly drew the wagons out of Bath yard, giving the impression that they had grease boxes almost frozen solid, then he dribbled along to the junction right up to the pegs; as he drew near, the bobby pulled them off. On the main line the Class 4F was still making heavy weather of it. He left her boxed up and hung his cap over the steam gauge. 'Don't look at it, kid, because it's not going to show; we'll wait until we hear the safety valves lift.'

Bob trundled the train along very gently on the first valve, past Long's Siding and Rudmore Park. Approaching the 1 in 121 Bitton Bank Bob had yet to put any coal on, or water in the boiler, and about a third showed in the glass. Bob said, 'I've got the "Back 'un" for Bitton, I'll see what I can sort out now. Open the doors.' The lad opened the firebox and Bob looked in. He took the firebar down and lifted the fire as much as he could and boxed her up. Boiler pressure was about 160 compared with 175 maximum.

Bob dropped the reverser two notches, looked at the boiler and thought, 'She'll stand that.' He opened the regulator full and hammered her from the second bridge at the bottom of the bank up through the cuttings to Oldland Common. Then he opened the firebox doors, fired and then shut her up again. They passed through Warmley with a pressure of about 140lb. 'Put the injector on now,' Bob said. 'we're approaching Mangotsfield North. Put the injector on and forget it. Don't shut it off, mind.' 'All right,' the lad replied. Bob deliberately crawled over the North Junction at approximately 10mph and soon as he was across he picked up the wagons again. When they reached the north end of Westerleigh yard Bob said, 'Shut that injector off,' as they had not gained much water and still only had about half a glass. 'Shut it off a minute.' Bob fired, boxed her up, dropped the reverser a couple of notches and opened the regulator further. Just approaching Yate signal-box the safety valves blew off and up went a column of steam. Bob said, 'On with that injector, we've won, I think'. Bob fired all the way to Gloucester. What interested Bob was that when he reached in his toolbox for something and turned round again, his young fireman had dapped over to Bob's side of the cab and was sitting on his seat, which was situated over the sector plate indicating cut-off, and was bringing the reverser up a turn. Bob inquired, 'What are you doing?' 'Oh,' he replied, 'I thought she was barking.' 'Never mind whether she's barking or not, it's nothing to do with you, you don't even know *your* job yet. Get back over to your own side!'

Persuading that Armstrong to make steam called for all Bob's expertise and road knowledge. He never had a moment to be nervous or to lack confidence at being in control for the first time. By the time they reached Tuffley Junction on the outskirts of Gloucester everything was fine, the fire had burnt through properly and the injector was on.

Class 4F 0–6–0 No. 4606 of 21D (Stratford-upon-Avon) at Gloucester, with the water column to the right of the smokebox. A cattle truck is behind the tender.

(June 1947 Roger Venning)

When they arrived at Gloucester Bob stopped exactly at the water column – and it was a work of art to stop there exactly at the right spot. His fireman put the bag in and Bob turned the water on. Only then did the Gloucester men emerge from the porters' room to relieve them; it was a cold morning, so they delayed coming out until the tender had been refilled. As Bob and his mate were about to step off the footplate, who should come striding down the platform with his black mac and bowler hat but Locomotive Inspector Jack Coombes. He called, 'Good morning, Robert' and received the reply, 'Good morning Mr Coombes.' 'Maiden voyage?' 'Yes.' 'Well, you'll remember it,' he said, 'it's D-Day, they've opened the Second Front.' Bob was so pleased at this news and the fact that he had reached Gloucester, that he forgot about the anxious time he had experienced earlier. His tea was still in the can on the tray above the firehole – he had been too preoccupied to drink it.

When Bob rang control and told them he was at Gloucester he was told, 'We've a train coming down and we want you to relieve the crew.' It was a 'Crab' with eighteen wagons for Bath. They climbed aboard and Bob noticed immediately that there was North coal in the tender. His young fireman was as happy as a sand-boy when he said, 'You can fire now, can't you? We need bags of steam.' 'I'll never shovel Welsh coal on a

GWR 4–6–0 No. 2927 *Saint Patrick* at Clifton Down station with a train of horse-boxes containing animals for the Royal Show. The turntable was located behind the locomotive's boiler. A 'Pannier' tank engine also stands in the yard.

(5.7.36 S. Miles Davey)

stationary engine again,' he said. 'I know now it's slow combustion coal.' Bob advised him to watch all the experienced men make their fire up. 'Stan Shellard used to level the fire left by the steam raiser and never put any on until the train was out in the yard. Even on the Dorset 7s he never used to throw lumps in. He built his fire as he went, and without a doubt Stan Shellard was the best fireman at Bath. He taught me how to fire like that and it's a very good idea. But most firemen make their fire up with lumps, then lift it after it's burnt through; but you mustn't lose the flame because if you do and then open the damper, it will go "Whoof" and explode on you – what we call a back-draught.'

Sometimes a fireman could have fun by keeping silent. One day George Usher was firing to Teddy Gardner. They were about to leave Bristol, Temple Meads, when Inspector George Arkwright from Gloucester came up and asked Teddy, 'Will the turntable at Clifton Down take a Class 4F 0–6–0, as Derby wants to know?' Teddy replied, 'Yes, I expect so, George.' Passing through Fishponds a few minutes later, Teddy Gardner turned to his fireman and reflected, 'I suppose I'm right about what I told Arkwright.' 'What was that?' his fireman queried. 'Didn't you hear what the inspector asked me at Temple Meads?' 'Oh,' he said, 'what was it?' But the fireman had, in fact, heard the conversation, and as a goods fireman shunting the yard knew that the turntable had actually been removed in 1932, the year before, and currently the space was utilised for coal storage.

Having passed as a driver, Bill Bagnall had to sign road cards so that the office staff knew which routes he was competent to drive over. Having worked over the line for five years, Bill was asked to sign for Leeds because he knew the road as well as anyone and had taken the trouble to write down the names of signal-boxes, to note those which had crossovers and had even made an itinerary to serve as a reminder whenever it was required. Nevertheless Bill refused to sign for the Leeds road because out of the six men who had been passed for driving, two had been in the Derby Link, with no chance of working to Leeds. All six had agreed only to sign for Derby so that those who had not been to Leeds would not be disadvantaged.

Running Shift Foreman Harry Moore pressed Bill to sign saying, 'Mark my words, William, you'll regret this action in the very near future because I can name the person who'll be the first to sign beyond Derby. You yourself have been many times to Leeds. If you're signing only to Derby, then you're saying that whilst firing on the roads beyond Derby, you took no notice of signals etc., or in other words "neglected your duties".' It was quite a speech. But Bill calmly said, 'I'll bet I could pass any questions on the road beyond Derby, but I must abide by the vote of the six, so that's that.' Harry knew better than to try to persuade Bill to change his mind.

One night Harry called Bill into his office – actually a hut where footplatemen booked on and off and the foreman's assistant dealt with most of the problems which arose. At the far end of this hut was Harry's private section – it had no door, just a frame where perhaps a door had once been. Harry called, 'Come and have a look at this, Bill.' So saying, he took down from a shelf the box containing the Board of Trade road cards of all passed firemen and drivers. He showed him the cards of the man who had proposed the unofficial agreement – and who had signed for *every* road which Bristol men ran over. Bill shocked Harry by asking, 'Who was the foreman who allowed this to happen?' 'Well,' said Harry, 'I can't stop a man signing, it's his responsibility.' Bill pointed out that the foreman also had the responsibility of checking that the man concerned had worked over the sections he was signing for.

The road learning system was built on the assumption that a driver had fired over a route – in other words had experienced engine working and thus had learned the gradients and had imprinted on his mind the road's layout. Then, travelling as a driver over those same roads, he would recall what he had learned and in bad weather or at night he would know almost exactly where he was and would be aware of where he would find the next signal. Counting overbridges and listening to lineside noises also indicated his whereabouts – for instance, travelling through a cutting would sound different from being in the open. Good drivers would impart such information to their mates.

The oldest passed firemen were placed on the shunters, but rarely ever did this job as 'Spare Book' working generally found them moved to cover 'spare work'. The eight eldest passed firemen, four on each shift starting at 6.00am and 2.00pm, were nearly always booked to cover a driver moved to 'more important work' in Barrow Road No. 2 or No. 3 link. No. 3 link drivers covered main line passenger vacancies – for example, the running of the double-headed Duke of Beaufort's Aintree special in 1935 required a set of men for the train engine and spare main line men for the assistant engine.

In the 1930s £3 12s was the weekly pay for first year drivers, followed by two annual rises each of 6s. £4 10s was only paid to a driver who had completed 313 main line turns, so it was quite possible for a driver who was unable for some reason to do main line work never to achieve the top payment of £4 10s for 48 hours' work. Men paid a mileage bonus only achieved it by satisfying two very important conditions: eyesight and an A1 physical standard, plus the necessary road knowledge; thus a decrease in a man's physical condition, or perhaps changing blood pressure, could cause him to be moved from main line work. Most drivers never reached the seniority to take them into the top links until the last few years of their working life. Those top link drivers were certainly skilled men. Take, for instance, a Bristol man with a road knowledge to Leeds. He was required to store in his head the location of some 700 signals, excluding ground signals; to know which side of the line 201 signal-boxes were placed and the approximate position of some 149 crossovers. All this knowledge was essential for the efficient and safe running of his train.

Bill Bagnall's initiation into taking part in representing men came after the 1926 General Strike. Several men were owed a week's wages, held up owing to the strike, and they were short of ready cash. One morning, at a picket assembled at the entrance to Barrow Road shed, Bill asked if anyone had been down the steps to the depot to inquire when they would receive their pay. He was informed that railway property was out of bounds to them, only non-strikers being allowed on it. Bold as brass, Bill went to the gate and down the steps to Shedmaster Gadsley Peet's office. His door was open so Bill knocked and asked if he could have a word with him.

Peet, immaculately dressed, asked who Bill was. He explained that he was one of the recently imported firemen from Birmingham and that being away from home they would like to know when the wages due to them would be paid. Peet replied, 'Ask Mr Burton to come and see me.' Bill started to go outside to get to the main office when Peet said, 'Go through that door.' Bill obeyed and noticed the surprised look on Burton's face as he stepped from the shedmaster's office with the message that Peet wished to see him. When Burton went into Peet's office he was asked, 'When are the wages being paid?' Burton replied, 'Friday, 12 noon.' Bill thanked Mr Peet and as he returned up the steps to the shed exit he saw dozens of heads looking over the wall. He gave the men the information they wanted and so ended Bill's first job as a representative.

Bill had cause to see Mr Peet again just after the strike had ended. Conditions were made that, as work demanded – and traffic did not quickly regain normal level – management would take on men in strict order of seniority. Bill's friend G. Millward had been called to work so Bill nipped down to the shed to find out if he, too, was wanted. Bill was most anxious not to miss his turn as he had already placed some of his personal effects in the care of a pawnbroker in nearby Church Road. Many of his colleagues had

BR Standard Class 5 4–6–0 No. 73138 at Barrow Road. The steps to the road can be seen on the left.
(August 1963 W.F. Grainger)

done the same. The foreman swore at him, and said that he would be fetched when required. Not satisfied with this reply, Bill went to Peet and asked the terms of restarting work. He was told, 'As work arises, so men will be taken on.' Bill answered, 'Then it's not as the foreman says.' 'What does he say?' Peet inquired, and was told the exact words, Bill adding, 'Begging your pardon.' 'Fetch him in here at once,' came the response. Bill went to the foreman's office and in a mild manner said, 'Mr Peet would like to see you, Foreman.' He reddened. 'Thee hasn't been and told him what I said?' 'Yes I have,' Bill retorted and followed him over to Peet's office. The foreman tried to close the door but Bill squeezed inside. Mr Peet rebuked the foreman for using strong language to 'a young lad on the threshold of his life on the railway', and Bill almost felt that a halo had been bestowed on him.

When Bill was reinstated after the 1926 Strike, he fired to Jimmy Taylor, a driver passed for goods work only, and was his mate for over three months until reorganisation of the links created a move. Bill soon discovered that Jimmy had to be handled gently, and discreetly directed to the correct course of action. If Jim said 'I think we ought to do x,'

Driver's-eye view of Westerleigh North signal-box.
(*c.* 1963 W.F. Grainger)

and Bill knew that it was impossible, he would say, 'Let's look at it as if an experienced driver was trying to do it.' They would then argue the case and decide on a sensible course of action. Bill found this procedure worked, settling the majority of the curious ideas which Jim entertained.

Bill well remembered one trip on the 7.40pm Bristol to Birmingham lodging turn. It was a Class B goods, which meant that it could take heavy traffic except for coal and iron ore. After Bristol it picked up wagons at Westerleigh, Coaley, Gloucester, Cheltenham and Bournville. It then called at Birmingham Central (at that period, it was the only train worked by Bristol men to call there) and finally New Street to pick up traffic for Lawley Street before the engine proceeded to Saltley shed, where the crew booked off after what was considered a hard night's work.

Arriving at Barrow Road shed early one evening they found that the engine allocated for the working was No. 3155, a former Class 2F 0–6–0 which had been re-boilered and upgraded to Class 3F. It had very low boxes on either side of the footplate which meant that there was no place for the crew to rest and so they had to stand throughout the trip. They found the engine on Ash Pit siding ready for them to prepare. Jimmy soon began his usual unpredictable behaviour, lifting up the well covers over the axle boxes – these covers were provided to protect the boxes from falling ash, etc. The covers could only be raised using a chisel passed between the spokes of a driving wheel. It was a really messy operation and one that was usually performed by shed staff using purpose-made tools, with a pump to draw off any water and a tube to refill the well. It was by no means part

The view of Tuffley Junction from the cab of a 'Crab' Class 5 2–6–0 working an Up stopping train.
(March 1964 W.F. Grainger)

Lawley Street goods depot, Birmingham.
(*c.* 1946 Author's collection)

of a driver's general preparation duty, but Jimmy had got a bee in his bonnet about them and decided that they must be attended to.

These wells were cast in the axle box, one on either side. A hole was drilled through the cast body of the unit which took a short plug-tailed trimming and Jimmy's fingers found one missing. It was not vital for the efficient working of the engine because the hole allowed sufficient oil to seep to the box side and so lubricate its riding on the horncheek, and as long as there was some oil in the well, the side of the box was lubricated. The more modern design had a three-pipe unit so that there was no need for the well at all, but some older axle boxes still used that type of casting. Now No. 3155 had a modern reservoir so the wells on the axle boxes were quite superfluous and could be ignored – but not by Jimmy, who moaned about drivers who neglected their preparation duties.

Bill was busy on the footplate, placing limestone in the firebox to prevent clinker forming on the firebars, when Jimmy bounded on to the footplate, his hands filthy from trying to squeeze them between the trailing wheel spokes. He took his Burton bag from the grub box bolted to the front of the tender. (The Burton bag was an oval leather container with a wood and leather flap to allow the carrying handles to pass through.) He then began to empty it, pushing its contents on to the low box that cornered the side of the footplate. This was soon covered with onions, packets of tea, sugar, tins of condensed milk, bread in a towel and, at last, the item he had been searching for, an old tobacco tin about 6in by 4in containing wire, corks, worsted for trimmings and a small pair of pliers. There were a few ready-made trimmings, but none of the required size for the axle keep trimming hole.

A passing friend, Driver Jack Beard (a character reputed to don an overcoat on 1 November and not remove it until 31 March), stopped to ask how he was, and Jimmy confided in him the dilemma of the trailing axle box with the missing trimming. Jack said, 'Don't bother, I'll get one out of my box,' for he, too, had a tobacco tin. 'You go round the engine and I'll see to the trimming for you.' With alacrity Jim accepted this kind offer, so the onions and other items that had been hastily pushed aside so that Jimmy could get at his trimming box were now whipped back into his bag without any thought of tidiness.

They eventually left the shed for the goods yard to back on to their train of some fifty wagons. The guard who gave them the loading was George Blackmore, whose son was a fireman at Barrow Road. Jimmy told Bill that he intended giving the box 'a bit of special attention', which Bill soon discovered meant pouring oil direct from the feeder down the central pipe.

Their first stop was at Westerleigh Sidings where Jimmy, shaking his oil bottle, found it almost empty. He told Bill, 'Look after her, I'm nipping down to the wagon examiner's cabin for some oil.'

There was an incline down to the cabin and bits of broken equipment often lay in that area. Jimmy, in his haste, tripped over a discarded coupling carelessly thrown down. He went one way and his 9-pint oil can the other. He returned to the engine with a grazed chin, rubbing it unhygienically with a wad of cotton waste, but with his 9-pinter full to the spout end. It was well known among enginemen who had studied oil and capillary action that the oil used on wagon axles was of little use for a locomotive's journal because more 'body' was needed. Jimmy, however, knew nothing of the finer aspects of lubrication – he just believed that oil was oil.

Class 4F 0–6–0 No. 44569 of 82E (Barrow Road) at Westerleigh Yard.
(*c.* 1963 W.F. Grainger)

When they left Westerleigh the spout of the full feeder was stuck into the central pipe and all the way to Gloucester Jimmy dosed the trailing box. They picked up traffic at Coaley, then ran down into Gloucester Yard where they put down and collected more wagons before proceeding a little further to Barnwood. As soon as they stopped Jimmy said, 'Now come down with me and feel her round.' This meant placing the back of a hand on each wheel boss to feel how warm it had become. They went down Jimmy's side, touched the trailing coupled wheel boss and found its temperature was normal. 'There,' Jimmy said, 'if I hadn't given it special attention, we might have had a hot box on our hands.' As he spoke he felt the driving wheel – and that really was hot! He quickly whipped his knuckles away. His expression was just like that of a child who had been smacked for being good.

The box had heated up because the trimmings to the main oil supply from the reservoir had to pass below the oil level; because they were below, sometimes, if not pressed fully home, they would greatly reduce the capillary action to almost nil.

Jimmy needed to get black oil down the main pipe to rectify the damage. Bill was left by himself to fill the tender with water while Jimmy walked to Gloucester locomotive

Class 2F 0–6–0 No. 3062 at Gloucester shed.
(21.3.53 Colin Roberts)

depot to fetch a supply of cylinder oil for the driving wheel. As black oil was really for cylinder use it was of tar-like consistency and had to be heated to get it to run down the pipe to the driving wheel bearing. Filling his oil can with this tacky oil made Jimmy even dirtier. When the oil was sufficiently hot he stepped along the framing and wedged the oil can into the pipe.

As they continued on their trip that night the axle box remained warm but, to give Jimmy his due, it certainly remained cooler than it had been at Gloucester. At each stop they made, Jimmy went along the framing and poured a feeder of cylinder oil down the main pipe.

Bill reminded Jimmy that on arrival at Saltley he would need to report the bearing defect so that the under-keep could be dropped and a new fitting inserted. Jimmy said, 'Yes, then they'll know that I saved a breakdown or an engine change.' Bill thought to himself, 'They'll also know that the trailing axle had had a bit of attention too.' No. 3155 was withdrawn in September 1928.

During the coal strike Jimmy and Bill were returning on a Saltley lodging turn. The 10.45pm Washwood Heath to Westerleigh was a mineral train, generally of coal. They signed on and found their engine in one of the three roundhouses at Saltley. The practice at the shed was for all engines not to be coaled and watered on arrival. Mounting the footplate they noticed that the tender was practically empty – just about a dozen shovelfuls of slack remained so Jimmy advised, 'Don't make up the fire with that stuff, wait till we've been to the coal stage. I'll do the shaft [the big ends and eccentric] you see to the sand and we'll finish her off outside.'

Blackwell, looking Down towards the head of the Lickey Incline.
(*c.* 1960 Lens of Sutton)

They duly arrived at the stage and there was Bill poised with a shovel ready to make up the fire as soon as the coal descended. 'Whoosh,' the first tubful came down. It was coke! Bill waited for the second tubful, thinking they were doing 'one and one' – that is, one of coke and one of coal. Then 'Whoosh', another load of coke descended. 'When's the coal coming?' Jimmy shouted, only to receive the reply, 'No coal up here.' 'Hold everything,' Jimmy instructed, and went to see the outside foreman, who allowed Bill and Jimmy to go to the coalstack roads and take just enough to make up their fire. They proceeded down the dark siding and Jimmy stopped as soon as he came to the large lumps making the stack wall. He was soon hurling them on the footplate, telling Bill to throw them in the tender. But with the firebox loaded, the damper shut and an appreciable amount of coal thrown on to the coke in the tender, the outside foreman arrived and terminated Jimmy's efforts. They set off to Washwood Heath to collect their train. They were banked up the 1 in 85 gradient to Camp Hill, where Jimmy yelled at the signalman 'Send him through,' meaning that he wanted the banker flagged (or rather, as it was night, lamped) up the 1 in 108 bank to King's Heath.

They encountered no steaming problems and just before reaching Blackwell the train was 'put inside' to allow another train to overtake. Jimmy took this opportunity to look

Bromsgrove, looking Down. The water column is at the far end of the platform on the left.
(*c.* 1960 Lens of Sutton)

at his train and returned with the information that the fourth wagon contained coal, its destination Torquay. Now a notice had been posted in the shed informing drivers that should they run short of coal they could take some from the wagons on the train, but they were to report the fact and say how much was removed.

Jimmy was anxious to take advantage of this ruling and so moved some coal first to the lap-plate between engine and tender, and then into the tender itself. Eventually they cleared Blackwell and took on water at Bromsgrove. At Spetchley they 'went inside' again, which gave Jimmy another opportunity to extract coal from the Torquay-bound wagon. Between them they managed to get about three lap-plate fulls into the tender. Carrying the coal was a dirty operation, but the fact that they could burn coal rather than coke overcame any distaste.

At Bredon, when an engine was turned into the loop, the guard was required to throw over a lineside lever to inform the signalman that it was clear for him to operate the release lever. The guard then changed the points and when the whole of the train was safely in the siding, the guard returned the points and the signalman relocked the road for the main line.

When they were inside this loop the guard, Harry Philpotts, was enlisted to help replenish the lap-plate. He and Jimmy found a wheelbarrow in a platelayers' cabin. Suddenly Bill heard a crash – Harry and Jimmy had dropped the door of the coal wagon, and were soon bringing barrow-loads to throw on the lap-plate for Bill to throw in the tender. They were in that loop for the best part of an hour and when their signal was

Bredon, looking Down. The goods loop where Bill, Jimmy and Harry re-coaled their engine is on the left at the far end of the platform.

(*c.* 1960 Lens of Sutton)

eventually pulled off, the three had great problems closing the wagon door against the weight of coal.

The rest of the trip to Westerleigh was easy as there was plenty of coal and coke. After uncoupling at Westerleigh Harry came to the footplate to ride down to Bristol. He told Bill and Jimmy, 'I've been into the cabin and had a wash because I looked as though I'd done the firing from Brum!'

On arrival at Barrow Road, while making out his report, Jimmy said, 'How much coal did we take from that wagon?' Not wishing to commit himself Bill replied, 'What's your judgement?' He replied, 'I think about 10cwt.' 'Oh,' said Bill, 'we ought to make it more than that, because if we only needed that amount, the gaffer will think that we could have made it without taking any at all.' Jimmy saw his point and said, 'Yes, we'll be generous. Put down 30cwt.' Bill said, 'Well Jimmy, that coal saved me a lot of hard work and you and Harry did a good job at Bredon. We ourselves don't have to pay – give 'em another ton,' so 2 tons 10cwt was entered in the report which Bill anticipated would please the Torquay coal factor.

Chapter Five

RAILWAY EXPERIENCES IN THE SECOND WORLD WAR

Railways were vital to the British war effort but, owing to the large amount of traffic, the shortage of staff and bombing, their operation was not always as efficient as in peacetime. Train-loads of petrol were hauled from Avonmouth to the areas where airfields were situated. After the fuel had been discharged, the transit labels on the wagon solebars were reversed to read 'Empty' and the tanks returned to the port.

One day Driver Bill Bagnall and his fireman Doug Jones left Westerleigh Sidings with thirty-nine empty tanks for Avonmouth headed by a Class 3F 0–6–0, not a type particularly renowned for its brake power. As the train moved away, Bill noticed that it seemed to drag somewhat and attributed this to the fact that Guard Jack Summerfield had not released his brake soon enough. On the undulating line towards Mangotsfield Bill experienced the feeling of pulling something more than thirty-nine empty tanks – which were usually good runners as they were well maintained. Adverse signals were sighted at Fishponds, and when they came to a stand, the thump felt on the footplate suggested that the guard had failed to use his brake.

The signalman warned Bill of a stop ahead at Kingswood Junction, so Bill carefully took his train down the gradient of 1 in 63–97. The 'bobby' there informed him that single line working was in operation between Kingswood Junction and Ashley Hill Junction. The pilotman sent them on to Stapleton Road Gas Siding signal-box where they were informed that an unexploded bomb had been found by Wee Lane (now Glenfrome Road) Bridge and that they were to proceed at 5mph to avoid making vibrations which might set the bomb off. After they had passed, at some distance, the unexploded bomb and the soldier guarding its sand-bagged crater, the Class 3F had insufficient impetus to climb the 1 in 73 gradient to Narroways Bridge carrying the LMS across the GWR's Lawrence Hill to Filton line. Bill decided that the only thing to do was to set back and take a smarter run at the incline. This entailed passing the unexploded bomb twice more: once in reverse and once going forward. The soldier's face expressed surprise at these several appearances, but even at a faster speed the engine failed to get up the bank.

Bill was just about to set back for a third attempt when Fireman Doug Jones, who was looking back, exclaimed excitedly, 'There's another engine behind us!' Bill said, 'How can there be another engine behind us when we're on single line working?' Bill was unaware that Stapleton Road Gas Siding signal-box had informed Kingswood Junction that the train of empty tanks had passed his box, so Kingswood had allowed a light engine at 'Caution' to travel as far as Stapleton Gas Siding outer home signal. In the

Fishponds station, looking Up.
(21.4.60 Author)

A Class 4P 4–4–0 Compound passes Kingswood Junction, Bristol, with a stopping passenger service to
Gloucester.
(April 1956 W.H. Harbor/Author's collection)

Signalman V.A. Frost looks out of Stapleton Road
Gas Works signal-box.
(1924 Author's collection)

course of setting back his train of thirty-nine empty tank wagons, Bill was getting near
this light engine. Doug yelled, 'Two trains on a single line ain't allowed!' Sensibly,
though, the light engine was utilised to push them over the summit at Narroways Bridge
where the banker dropped off.

Bill's engine pulled to a dead stand on the rising gradient of 1 in 77 in Montpelier
Tunnel and again Driver George Millward and his light engine provided assistance from
behind. On the rising 1 in 75 between Redland and Clifton Down the Class 3F stalled
again and this time a GWR 0–6–0PT from Montpelier assisted in the rear to Clifton
Down where Bill was informed that Control had ordered the Clifton Down 0–6–0PT to
pilot him to Avonmouth. They descended through Clifton Down Tunnel on a gradient
of 1 in 64 and touched at least 50mph in the dip through Sea Mills station, but, even so,
they only just managed to master the 1 in 100 rise at Horse Shoe Bend.

On arrival at Avonmouth the head shunter, 'Caggy' Grey – called 'Caggy' because he
was left-handed – came up to Bill asking, 'What sort of a load do you reckon to have
here?' Bill replied, 'A train of empty tanks' – and was startled to hear Caggy exclaim,
'Empty, my foot, they're all loaded and total about 55 of mineral!' – which equalled
about three train-loads for a Class 4F engine. No wonder she had struggled!

Meanwhile, the soldier on guard duty at Wee Lane reported to the military authorities
that a crazy engine driver was see-sawing his train over the area where the unexploded
bomb was situated. In due course this message was relayed back to Control – where staff

Looking towards Kingswood Junction from the cab of a Class 4F 0–6–0 at Stapleton Road Gas Works sidings.
(*c.* 1963 W.F. Grainger)

Class 4F 0–6–0 No. 44266 at Stapleton Road Gas Works.
(*c.* 1955 W.H. Harbor/Author's collection)

Class 1P 0–4–4T No. 1397 leaves Montpelier Tunnel heading a Clifton Down to Bournemouth West train comprising SR stock.
(18.4.36 S. Miles Davey)

were beginning to accept that the psychiatric assessment by the soldier might be quite accurate in view of the reports coming in on the happenings to a train of empty tanks en route from Westerleigh to Avonmouth. All was explained when it was reported that thirty-nine tank loads of aviation spirit which should have been unloaded at Liverpool had indeed arrived at their destination – but then were returned as 'empties'.

One night when Bob Ford was firing for Driver Ralph Holden on the Bath to Birmingham parcels train, they were just north of Eckington and approaching Defford when German raiders dropped a bomb in a field about 150yd from the engine, so Bob knew the enemy raiders were above and could hear the distinctive pulsing of their aero-engines. It was the fireman's job to set the plug on the steam heat gauge to give a pressure of about 50lb psi, but in the blackout and because Bob had been busy, the needle on the steam heat pressure gauge had crept up without him noticing.

It was broad moonlight when they drew up at King's Norton to unload milk churns. They had blackout sheets all round the cab to hide any glare from the firebox and they

Redland, looking towards Clifton Down. The footbridge is an attractive design befitting its situation in a residential area.

(1960 Lens of Sutton)

could still hear the German aircraft circling overhead. Ralph Holden said, 'Don't get opening those firebox doors, mind. We don't want them to see us' – though even if Bob had done so it would not have made much difference as the moonlight was bright enough to read by. Ralph continued, 'I wonder what those porters are doing back there with the milk. I'll go back and see. I don't want to stay here long.' Saying this, he left the cab and swiftly strode along the platform.

Alone, Bob glanced round the cab to make sure all was well and noticed that the steam heat gauge showed 90lb psi, so he quickly turned it down. When Ralph returned he said, 'What do you think? That milk's so hot they can't handle the churns!' All innocence, Bob inquired, 'How did that happen, then?' 'Well,' Ralph said. 'We're not staying here any longer. I told them to shut the doors and we'll take the churns to Brum and if they like they can send them back to King's Norton in the morning. I'm certainly not staying here to be bombed.'

As soon as they got the Right Away from King's Norton Ralph said, as he always did, 'Come on, take over the driving.' He had previously asked Bob to wash the bucket out

The view from Clifton Down station down the gradient of 1 in 64 to the tunnel mouth.
(May 1954 Dr A.J.G. Dickens/Author's collection)

The Horse Shoe Bend, showing (from right to left): the River Avon; the Bristol to Avonmouth railway; and
the contractor's temporary track for building the Portway, now the A4, a new and shorter road between
Bristol and Avonmouth.
(c. 1924 Author's collection)

BR Standard Class 9F 2–10–0 No. 92000 of 82E (Barrow Road) at the Royal Edward Yard, Avonmouth, with a train of tanks containing diesel oil for Birmingham buses.
(August 1964 W.F. Grainger)

and put warm water in. Off came Ralph's slop, cap, collar and tie. He washed his hands and face, replaced his collar, tie, cap and slop – and by this time they were at Five Ways between the two tunnels, creeping down into New Street. Then he said, 'Come on, I'll take over and you wash.' Bob did not bother to wash his face because it did not feel dirty, but he cleaned his hands and then packed his bags ready for relief when another crew took over.

For their return working, Ralph and Bob relieved the crew of the Down Leicester parcels at New Street's No. 4 platform, officially the No. 6 Down platform for passengers. On the left, under a high wall, was a siding known as the Mortar Mill. In it were two parcels vans which they had to pick up and place on the front of their train. The signal-box was about 30yd from them, across to the right. The signalman's own personal air raid shelter looked like a Dalek – a dome-shaped iron affair with a door. Bob said that he would not have been anxious to use it and would have preferred taking refuge in the tunnel which was only a few yards away.

Eckington, looking Up.
(*c.* 1960 Lens of Sutton)

Defford, looking Up.
(*c.* 1905 Author's collection)

Birmingham New Street. On the left is the LNWR station built in 1854, and on the right the MR station, built in 1885.
(*c.* 1905 Author's collection)

Ralph drew the parcels train forward over the points in the tunnel before setting back to collect the vans. Surrounded by their own smoke and steam, with glands blowing, the injector valve blowing and visibility almost nil, Bob climbed down the cab steps to look at the disc signal from ground level to check that it had been pulled 'off' to indicate that the points had changed. At the same time Bob was listening hard because the shunter could not indicate by visible signals so he was expected to sound a code on his horn: a single blast meant go ahead; two blasts come back; three blasts stop; and four blasts ease couplings.

Bob and Ralph waited in the tunnel for 10 minutes. Bob made sure that the safety valves would not lift because it was almost a dismissal offence to blow off in New Street station as the Queen's Hotel, owned by the LMS, stood just above that wall by the Mortar Mill and a violent escape of steam would have disturbed sleeping guests. Bob, standing on the ground beside his engine, called to Ralph, 'There's something wrong.' They knew the German raiders were still around because they could hear bombs exploding.

Bob walked back to the tunnel portal. No one seemed to be about. He looked hard but could see no sign of the signalman in his box. Bob shouted . . . but received no response whatever, so their train had to stay in the tunnel because the disc signal was against them. 'Have a Woodbine, Bob,' said Ralph. 'We're safe here.'

Eventually a fair-haired shunter came along. Bob knew his face quite well and on one occasion he had thrown a Swiss roll into the tender, calling out, 'Here you are, there's no need to starve when I'm about.' This shunter told Bob and Ralph, 'There's a lot of trouble back there, they've dropped a bomb in the Mortar Mill. Those parcels vans are gone for a Burton; probably half the wall's gone – there's at least 30ft down – but you can't tell for certain yet because there's too much smoke, dust and rubble.' Bob said, 'What's going to happen then? Is the main line all right?' 'As far as I know,' came his reply. 'Where's the bobby?' inquired Bob. 'Oh, he's in his shelter.' 'Well, fetch him out, get him back in his box and tell him to get us back on our train. As we're not able to go in the Mortar Mill now, we want to get out of Brum immediately.'

With the utmost difficulty the shunter persuaded the scared signalman to leave his shelter, enter his box, pull the points, move the disc and allow them to set back on to their train. The shunter coupled them up and Bob said to Guard Reg Moore, a Bath man, 'Jump into the van as quickly as you can, Reg, we're getting out of here as soon as we can hit the trail.' Bob told Ralph, 'We'll chance what steam and fire we have, blow for the peg and let's go.' The bobby pulled the signal off and almost immediately Bob saw him racing down the steps back to his shelter. Bob said to Ralph, 'Go like the clappers and get away from this lot.' Ralph opened the regulator and they were soon in the tunnel and in due course reached home safely, without further excitement. Altogether Ralph and Bob shared about a dozen Birmingham blitzes.

Either late in 1939 or early in 1940 Bob was on shed relief one Sunday morning disposing and preparing engines with a mate. It was 10.30am and he had been on duty for about 1½ hours when Tom Rudd, the running shed foreman, came out and said, 'Bob, we've just got orders from Control. It's the first I've heard of it, but there's a troop special coming up the Dorset. Slip home and get a lodging basket, it'll be here in about an hour.' Bob was by then a passed cleaner. He nipped home to Great Stanhope Street, about 5 minutes' walk from the shed, collected a twopenny tin of Nestlé's milk, tea, sugar, bread and cheese sandwiches and bread and banana sandwiches. The basket packed, he said to his wife, 'Don't know when you'll see me, I don't know where we're going,' and with that he returned to the shed. Tom said, 'Got your basket?' and when Bob answered in the affirmative he continued, 'Well go and get No. 1000, that's the one you're to have. It's out there.' Class 4P Compound No. 1000 was a 'foreigner', not a Bath engine.

Bob had only been on her for about 5 minutes, filling the sand bins and trimming the lamps, when who should arrive but the 'Gable Kid'. His name was Leonard Freer, and he was later to leave the railway and open an antique shop in Charles Street, very close to Green Park station. Extremely good-looking, he had a Clark Gable moustache and eyes, making him the glamour boy of the shed. Aged about 37, he was a nice fellow. He greeted Bob with, 'Here, what's this job then?' Bob replied, 'I don't know, you've got a route card haven't you?' 'No,' he replied. 'I haven't a card, but it's coming in from

Second World War posters requesting passengers to limit rail travel to essential journeys so that the railways could give priority to war supplies.
(Author's collection)

Class 4P 4–4–0 Compound No. 1000 preserved at the Transport Museum, Clapham Common.
(*c.* 1964 R.J. Cannon/Author's collection)

Bournemouth – a special, and it's bound to have a number on the front.' Bob said, 'All right, I'll go and get the number for it'. When they had finished preparing the engine they booked off shed and stood No. 1000 under the station signal-box.

About 11.45am the train drew in with about ten coaches on, a double-header manned by Bournemouth men. The disc came off, they took No. 1000 forward, then backed down and coupled up. They were still quite unaware of their destination. The guard said 'Birmingham' and told them the tonnage. 'Then he walked two coach lengths away from the engine, came back and added, 'These blokes reckon they're going to Llandudno.' Bob said, 'Well we aren't going to Llandudno because we don't know the road unless they fix us up with pilots.' Len said, 'Brummagem is as far as I'm taking them.' The signal fell and off they went.

They made good time with No. 1000, the engine going well, and in due course they pulled alongside Ryecroft Motive Power Depot, which Bob had not seen since he had transferred to Bath. Len said to him, 'We're picking up a pilot' and soon Jimmy Lote, a driver previously well known to Bob in his days at Walsall, climbed on to the footplate. He saw Bob and said, 'What are you doing here?' Then he looked at handsome Len and exclaimed, 'Blimey, they must all be good-looking at Bath.' He then went on to say, 'I've got to pilot you to Wolverhampton.' Bob asked why they were going there, but Jimmy didn't know. 'Those are my orders, Bob; all I know is I've got to pilot you to Wolverhampton.' Len said, 'Don't worry, Bob, you've done enough from Bath to here. Jimmy can drive and I'll fire.' Jimmy agreed to this suggestion. Jimmy was a North Western man and although Bob had seen 'Royal Scots' and 'Baby Scots' at Ryecroft he had never seen a Compound there, so it might well have been the first time Jimmy had handled one.

They left Ryecroft and went towards Wolverhampton, all work against the collar. Len let the water in the boiler get high and approaching Wolverhampton Jimmy Lote had to close the regulator for an adverse signal. Despite this No. 1000 was still pulling and Jimmy rightly looked concerned. Len asked, 'What's the matter with you? Is it shut?' 'She's down all right.' Len suggested, 'Open the taps if you don't know and see whether she's blowing steam out.' The trouble was that water had entered the main pipe to the steam chest, and although Jimmy Lote was a competent driver, he was dealing with an unfamiliar machine. Len suggested, 'Open the regulator and then slam it again.' Jimmy did so, and the engine came under control. They rolled into Wolverhampton and Jimmy said, 'Well, this is as far as I go. Nice to see you, Bob. Cheers,' – and was gone.

There they stood at Wolverhampton. Len was unfamiliar with the road while Bob had at least travelled from Wolverhampton to Crewe but could hardly claim to know the route – and in any case it was the driver who had to sign for road knowledge. A well-built man then appeared carrying a tin box bearing his name, Ben Hiatt, and explained that he had orders to pilot the train to Crewe. They welcomed him aboard, and about 5 minutes later received the Right Away from Wolverhampton to Crewe. Time was getting on – it was 2.30 or thereabouts – and Bob was beginning to feel that he had had enough. Nevertheless he found strength enough to fire No. 1000 to Crewe. As they drew up at a platform there he said to Len, 'I don't know about you, I know we're supposed to lodge, but *where* are we going to lodge? And if we're going to lodge, when are we going to be relieved?'

Len rang Control, and explained that they had come all the way from Bath, and said that so far they had had two pilots, that they were complete strangers to the road and thought they deserved to be relieved. He added that they did not even know the train's destination, though the soldiers on board reckoned they were going to Llandudno. Control, unhelpfully, said it was a Sunday so they had no spare men and therefore could provide no relief.

Len was a dogmatic type and master of his job. He asked for Bob's opinion. Bob said, 'Well, as far as I'm concerned, I'll make a hole in the fire to stop it raising steam; shut the damper; fill the boiler up and leave it, train and all, and go back home travelling as a passenger. That's how I feel, Len.' Len rang Control again and told them bluntly, 'We're not going any further, you can do what you like about it. We'll leave the train with the blower shut off, a hole in the fire, we'll close the dampers and fill the boiler up out of sight, then we're catching the first passenger back to Bath because we've had enough.'

True to their word they caught a passenger train and rode home, the journey taking about 5 hours. They were unable to catch a connection at Mangotsfield at that time of day on a Sunday so had to travel to Temple Meads, take a train to the Bath GWR station and then walk to the LMS shed to book off. They put in about 12½ hours that day. Tom Rudd had gone off duty by then but his deputy, Dick Tidball, who was also a driver, commented that he would have done the same if he had been in their boots. Fortunately they never heard anything further.

It was not unknown for a driver or fireman to endure bombing at Bristol; then suffer another raid elsewhere during his lodging turn rest period, followed by yet another raid when he returned home. The constant danger caused footplate crews to refuse lodging turns – and this led to trouble. They were hauled up before Harry Whitaker, the District Locomotive Superintendent for the Bristol, Gloucester, Bath, and Somerset & Dorset area. (Interestingly, he was the son of Alfred Whitaker, the S&D's former locomotive superintendent.) As there were so many offenders, Whitaker had to take their complaints seriously and he contacted Derby. This resulted in a meeting at Bath where Colonel Harold Rudgard, the Line Superintendent, was to inquire into the worse cases that the men could place before him. One Bristol man asked Bill Bagnall what he thought the outcome of the meeting would be. Bill knew that Rudgard was a fair man, but footplatemen were certainly 'refusing duty', which was a very serious offence. If Rudgard agreed, Bill offered to attend the meeting in his capacity as the local representative of the Associated Society of Locomotive Engineers and Firemen.

Bill arranged to be off duty for the time of the meeting and obtained a privilege ticket to travel from Temple Meads to Bath via the GWR. Bill duly boarded the train at Temple Meads. Unknown to him, Harry Whitaker was also on board. When the stopping train called at Oldfield Park, a Bath suburban station, Bill was surprised to see Whitaker step off. Guessing where he was going, Bill nipped out too. He followed him along a cinder path and down Brougham Hayes and was surprised when Whitaker turned round and said, 'Hello, Bagnall, where're you going?' Bill replied, 'I was following you, sir. I presume you're meeting Colonel Rudgard at the loco shed, and seeing you get out at Oldfield Park, I decided there was no need to go right on into Bath.' 'Yes,' Whitaker said, 'this is the nearest station.'

Whitaker mentally ticked off the names of those due to meet Rudgard. Then he turned and said, 'You're not one of the men on the list.' Bill confirmed that and continued, 'I'm going to see if Colonel Rudgard will see me, because I'm ASLEF's local representative.'

They arrived together at Bath MPD. The chief clerk there, Mr Blackshaw, had previously served at Barrow Road and so was already known to Bill. He agreed to ask permission for Bill to see Rudgard. When Bill entered the room he saw Rudgard seated at the table, with an officer on either side of him. Behind these three was Mr Whitaker; also seated was a male secretary taking notes. Facing the table was a row of chairs. Blackshaw ushered the locomen in and they sat facing Rudgard, who presented a preamble stating the reason for the meeting. He explained that because of the war Parliament had passed an Act removing freedom of choice regarding working conditions. Railways were a very important part of the war effort and it was left to the good sense of railway workers to carry on under conditions that normally would not be tolerated. He said that he was responsible for making sure the LMS fully carried out its share of the war

An Up stopping train leaves Oldfield Park Platform.
(26.8.54 Author)

effort and he could be called to account should any delays occur. This was why he wanted to hear why the men were refusing duty.

The first to speak was Teddy Tanner, whose principal problem was the long hours on the trip between Bristol and Birmingham. Owing to delays on his outward goods journeys, he failed to catch most of his return rostered workings. This meant that he was never certain when he would be home and so was unable to make suitable arrangements for his wife. Alone in the house, she was frightened during the air attacks. If they knew that he was going to be absent overnight, she usually made arrangements to stay with her sister, who lived some distance out of Bristol. Next to speak was Ern Pullen. He reported that he was once away from home for so long that his wife rang the loco shed and then, as he still did not appear, she went there in person. She was concerned that something might have happened and that he could be lying somewhere dead or seriously hurt. The third speaker was Art Groves, who objected to taking rationed food from his family because this action had caused family arguments. Two other men spoke and they were followed by Art Garrard, ASLEF's local secretary, who revealed that he had a disabled daughter, who needed assistance to reach the air raid shelter.

It was then Bill's turn to speak. 'My trouble is very similar to yours, sir.' This surprised Rudgard, who asked him to explain what he meant. Bill said that he was the local representative of these and other men, and as he could find no easy answers to their problems, he had come to the meeting to hear what Rudgard had to say. Rudgard, experienced in debate, turned the tables on Bill by asking him, 'You know the situation. What, in your opinion, should or could be done?'

Bill replied, 'There are three factors that need attention.' As he said this, Rudgard gave the secretary at the end of the table a meaningful look which clearly meant, 'Get this down.' Bill's, first point was that the three booked turns of lodging work per week should be reduced to one. Secondly, to ease the long hours on the road, relief points should be established between Bristol and Birmingham – perhaps sited at Ashchurch and Bromsgrove. Thirdly, that food should be issued to men on lodging work.

In reply, Rudgard suggested that the links should be arranged between the men and Mr Whitaker. Established relief points needed the approval of the Sectional Council as it involved a certain amount of promotion. Regarding food, Rudgard said he was not a free agent, but he would do what he could. He thanked the men and asked them to bear with the management, which was trying to cope with many problems.

The outcome of the meeting was that Rudgard enabled all three points to be acted on in accordance with the men's wishes. The Local Departmental Committee arranged one lodging turn per week; two sets of relief men were based at Ashchurch and Bromsgrove; and tins of sausages, sardines and soup were issued to men on lodging turns.

After the meeting Rudgard approached Bill. He had noticed that the six other men were in railway uniform (and therefore had free travel), but Bill was not and he now inquired how he had travelled from Bristol to Bath. Bill said that he had purchased a Privilege Ticket and was at that moment off-duty. Rudgard kindly advised that he could claim any reasonable cost for attending, but Bill thanked him and said that as it was his own idea to attend, no claim would be made. After leaving the meeting, the seven Bristol men found that two cans of tea were available for them in the Bath locomen's cabin, to encourage them to recount the events of the meeting.

In 1940 the order went out for 'Vans, vans, vans' to be sent to Avonmouth. Control tried all possible locations where these much sought-after vehicles might be stored. Banana traffic had ceased for the duration of the war and the use of banana vans at Avonmouth was therefore limited, so this demand for their use came as a surprise to railwaymen. At that time Avonmouth was receiving nightly visits from the Luftwaffe, which may have had information of ammunition ships arriving. The railway authorities devised a plan to get the ships' cargo unloaded into vans as quickly as possible and then as rapidly dispersed. It was an exercise with the highest priority, and it depended for success on having enough vans, engines and men available to move the trains from Avonmouth to any part of the country.

Area Controls were instructed to dispatch vans to Avonmouth as soon as possible. The Sheffield area managed to assemble a train of fifty-nine vans and an engine was immediately ordered from Millhouses MPD. The shed rose to the occasion and turned

Ashchurch: the Evesham branch platform, looking south towards the Birmingham to Gloucester line.
(*c.* 1960 Lens of Sutton)

out its star 4–4–0 Compound No. 1079, and the train was soon on its way to Avonmouth.

Saltley Control had the task of finding staff to take the train forward – and discovered in its lodging house a set of Bristol locomen and a guard. The home shed was contacted to check on Driver Bagnall's road knowledge, because between Gloucester and Yate alternative routes were available over which the train could be directed. Saltley was informed that the driver named had the road knowledge to take his train over whichever route he was directed, so the three Bristol men were told to book on and obtain their instruction from the shed foreman.

On arrival at the shed they were told to walk to Saltley station, relieve the crew arriving from Sheffield and take the train on to Avonmouth. At the station they found No. 1079, its huge train of empty vans and a brake. After a brief exchange of words, the guard, Jack Summerfield, said that it was a fully-fitted train, so in order to let the footplate crew know when he had arrived at his van, he would touch the brake setter. The Millhouses men told the new footplate crew that the engine was special and would do anything required of it.

A rake of banana vans at Avonmouth.
(*c.* 1947 Author's collection)

As soon as the vacuum gauge indicated that the guard had reached his van, the enginemen were ready to set off, with a banker assisting them to King's Heath. Saltley Control informed Duddeston Road signal-box that this train should have priority running and as far as possible should be given a clear run over the whole of its journey. The signals came off and the special moved up the slip road, by-passing a goods train waiting to proceed up the Camp Hill line. Lawley Street Junction signal-box offered an unimpeded run and the distant signal for Brickyard Crossing did likewise. The train was proceeding at a reasonable speed as it came to the steepest part of the run, the 1 in 85 climb from Bordesley Junction to Camp Hill. Bill, who had much experience with Compounds, having fired for years on the Bristol to Derby, Sheffield and Leeds expresses, soon realised that he had an exceptional tool in No. 1079. Speed increased through Brighton Road and the tunnel before King's Heath. Hazelwell passed almost in a flash, then, below the two Lifford homes, were two distant signals for King's Norton, the right-hand one displaying green, indicating that there they were to be turned on to the main line. This came about through the signalman at King's Norton calling Control

Saltley station.
(1968 D. Payne)

and asking which train should be given priority, as he had this special and an express that had left New Street. Control instructed him to favour the special. This 'tip' was passed from box to box, mainly by word of mouth.

Progress of the special was 'clocked' and its progress reported to Control. Northfield and Barnt Green came and went. As the train was fully fitted it was not required to stop at the head of the Lickey Incline for the brakes to be pinned down. Since on one occasion a train had overcome its braking power on the 1 in 37½ gradient, all trains were now required to have a clear run through Bromsgrove before being allowed to leave Blackwell. Control had asked both Blackwell and Bromsgrove boxes to offer Line Clear, and as the special ran through Barnt Green station the tall distant signal was 'off' for

Northfield, looking Up.
(*c.* 1910 Author's collection)

Blackwell – which meant that the special had a clear road to Stoke Works Junction. Express passenger trains were expected to take a minimum of 5 minutes for the 2½-mile long incline, there being a 20mph restriction at Blackwell and 30mph at Bromsgrove. Bill took No. 1079 down at the same speed as an express, released the brakes passing through Bromsgrove station and had accelerated to 40mph by Bromsgrove South. Taking advantage of the gradient of 1 in 283 down, the special ran through Stoke Works Junction at its maximum speed of 60mph. No. 1079 was running perfectly, with the low pressure needle standing firmly on 30lb psi and the big double-handed regulator almost closed.

At Dunhampstead the signalman had just welcomed his friend, an off-duty police constable, into the signal-box. They usually played a game or two of cribbage together, lubricating their throats with a flagon of scrumpy. The signalman told his companion, 'Just listen to this train now coming.'

Bill remembered very accurately the timing of the expresses he had fired on for so many years. They were allowed 15 minutes to pass Dunhampstead and clear Ashchurch, 17½ miles distant. He realised that No. 1079 could equal this timing, despite the fact that

View up the 1 in 37½ gradient from Bromsgrove.
(16.4.53 Dr A.J.G. Dickens/Author's collection)

instead of eighty wheels to turn in axleboxes there were three times that number behind this Compound. Bill glanced at his watch and put the engine to work a little harder as they approached Dunhampstead, judging that they were doing well over 60mph. The game of cribbage took a back seat for a few moments as the special flashed by the box. The signalman rang Abbot's Wood Junction and the conversation went, 'Joe, there's one coming down, let's track him, eh?' At Abbot's Wood Junction the signaller answered, 'All right Fred, I'll call Albert at Ashchurch.'

All this went on behind the scenes as the special roared on. At Abbot's Wood Junction a GWR fitted freight from Worcester had been brought to a stand, its fireman in the signal-box carrying out Rule 55, which every engineman had drilled into him. 'What are we waiting for?' the GWR fireman asked. 'We shan't stop anything.' The signalman told him that a special was taking precedence and that even if his train had a light over each buffer – indicating an express passenger train – he would still have to wait there until the special had passed through.

Class 2P 4–4–0 No. 509 with a Birmingham to Gloucester train near Abbot's Wood Junction.
(*c.* 1935 Colin Roberts collection)

The Compound soon roared by at about 70mph. Pirton Sidings and Defford boxes both kept the road clear. The distant was on at Eckington, a notorious stopping point because of the level crossing there, but was pulled off as they passed under the road bridge at Defford. The special proceeded a long the straight track to Bredon and Ashchurch. Meanwhile, back at Abbot's Wood Junction, on the footplate of the engine heading the GWR fitted freight, the disbelieving Worcester driver was saying, 'And you say the bobby said that even if we had a lamp on each buffer, we'd still have to wait until that special went by?' His fireman replied, 'Yes, and the phones were ringing and he had to report to whoever it was on the other end.' The driver continued, 'Mate, we're seeing history tonight, but because of the need for wartime secrecy, I doubt if we'll ever hear the reason, or find out what was so special about that train. I've never seen vans run like that anywhere! They're supposed to be limited to 60mph, but if I know anything, he was certainly touching 70.'

On the special they saw the Ashchurch distant signal pulled clear and they passed the box on the platform with the signalman working his bells. He also rushed to the 'ticker' and sent 'clear' to Bredon while Dunhampstead called him on the phone for news of the

View from the cab of BR Standard Class 9F 2–10–0 No. 92151 at Cheltenham Spa (Lansdown), showing
the water column on the Down platform.

(1964 W.F. Grainger)

timing. The special whizzed through Cleeve, slowing through Cheltenham, High Street
and Alstone Junction before drawing to a stop at Cheltenham Lansdown's water crane.

Bill left his fireman to shut the water off while he went back to the signal-box on the
station platform and spoke to the signalman. 'Tell Control that if they're turning us
through Eastgate, we'll want a clear run.' Hearing this request, the bobby thought, 'If I
know anything, you'll get your through run, mate.'

The tender tank filled and the signal remaining off, away went the special again. The
few passengers on the platform watched the train pull away and remarked on its length
and the uniformity of the vans in its formation. Meanwhile it was decision time for
Gloucester Control. With a GWR goods train somewhere south of Tuffley Junction, it
was decided to send the special through Gloucester Eastgate as the LMS tracks south of
Gloucester were clear of trains.

Meanwhile the special passed Hatherley Junction, Cheltenham, and Churchdown; at
Engine Shed Junction, Gloucester, they saw the distant was off for Eastgate. Speed was

'Jubilee' Class 4–6–0 No. 45682 *Trafalgar* approaching Barton Street Junction signal-box with an Up stopping train.
(*c*. 1964 W.F. Grainger)

reduced to take Tramway Junction smoothly at 30mph. Seeing Barton Street Junction distant clear meant that California Crossing and Painswick Road Crossing were also clear, so speed was now increased to get a run at the 1 in 108 bank. As the special accelerated through Eastgate station, staff in Control drew back the blackout blinds in the office at the south end of the platform to watch it pass. Bill, realising the capabilities of his superb engine, even had her compounding passing California Crossing and was most surprised to find that she was easily going to pass the summit at Tuffley as gracefully and easily as if she had a nine-coach express behind. Naas Crossing and Haresfield were soon behind, and at Standish Junction the signalman was now aware why he had to keep a 'cross-lighter' (express freight) standing at his GWR signals. Stonehouse, Frocester and

'Crab' Class 5 2–6–0 No. 42900 of 2E (Saltley) at Haresfield with an Up stopping train. The two ex-GWR tracks are immediately beyond the fence on the left.
(March 1964 W.F. Grainger)

Coaley saw little of the sixty vehicles which sped by; then Berkeley Road and the automatic intermediate block signals at Wick indicated that Charfield was clear. In fact, they had cleared the road there by shunting a fitted goods. This action caused a pair of Bristol men to fume when they were informed that they had to wait to give precedence to a special.

Wickwar was soon lost in the smoke of the 1401yd-long tunnel, unlined for most of its length since it was blased out of solid limestone. The disused limekiln that marked the incline's summit was passed. At Yate they found out which route they would be given to Avonmouth when they saw clear signals for the line towards Mangotsfield.

Behind in the brake van, Jack Summerfield, who had marvelled at the clear road and the train's fast running, was now in a quandary. As the special had been routed via Westerleigh, was it there that the train should be reduced in length to conform with the regulations governing the Kingswood Junction to Avonmouth route which involved more restricted weights and train lengths than the route traversed so far? When he

BR Standard Class 5 4–6–0 No. 73013 draws into Coaley station with an Up stopping train. The top of
Driver Woodman's cap can be seen in the lower right-hand corner.
(19.10.63 W.F. Grainger)

observed Westerleigh North distant off, he was in two minds as to whether to stop the
train by lifting the brake setter in his van or simply let it run on. Before he could make
his decision they were already roaring between the Up and Down yards.

Mangotsfield North Junction signal-box and Station box were passed at just over
30mph. The right-hand distant signal below the Fishponds Starter was also 'off' – Bill
had never seen this signal 'off' before – and so the section from Kingswood Junction to
Ashley Hill was clear. The guard thought to himself, 'It's out of my hands now.' At
Ashley Hill Junction, however, the distant signal was 'on' for Montpelier and they came
to a stand for the first time since leaving Cheltenham. On the footplate the driver was of
the opinion that starting on the rising gradient of 1 in 76 would certainly be a test of the
Compound's capabilities.

Off came the signal. He opened the regulator and away they went. In fact, acceleration
was so good that by the time they were passing through Redland station, he slipped the

The view from Mangotsfield North Junction signal-box. The line to Bristol curves sharply to the right, while the line to Bath continues straight on.
(June 1961 G.R. Dent/Author's collection)

regulator over into compound position and that marvellous No. 1079 took them up the 1 in 79 and over the summit at Clifton Down. Guard Summerfield was impressed as they sped down the 1 in 64 in the 1751yd-long tunnel below the Downs, through Sea Mills and up the 1 in 100 at Horse Shoe Bend. Then they reached Shirehampton and the approach to Avonmouth, where they were diverted to the Long Road, adjacent to the Weighbridge Road. Certainly it had been a trip to remember.

On another occasion during the Second World War, when returning from Gloucester with a goods train, Bill was stopped at Yate and told by the signalman to shunt off all the trucks except for the loaded cattle wagons. Bill drew his train forward and then halted with the brake van at the signal-box so that the guard could also be informed of the action to be taken. The guard was 'Sailor' Dickinson, so called because he had spent some time in the navy. He planned to shunt his van to the Machine Road, place the unwanted vehicles in a siding, back the cattle vans on to his brake and then continue.

The planned moves were made correctly but just as Bill was about to 'whistle up' the signalman to tell him they were ready, 'Sailor' suddenly yelled, 'Whoa! Whoa!' Bill

Shirehampton station, looking towards Clifton Down.
(*c.* 1910 Author's collection)

climbed down from the cab and went back to him to discover the problem. Sailor said, 'There's a cow here with her leg hanging through the bottom of the wagon.' And sure enough Bill could see the protruding hoof. A floor plank was missing. Sailor, with his inventive turn of mind, went to the wagon repairers' shed round the back of the weighbridge hut and returned with a suitable plank to place over the gaping aperture.

As Sailor approached the wagon and was about to drop the lower of the three doors, Bill, thinking ahead, said, 'Half a mo'. If you do that, those cattle are going to think they're being released.' But Sailor was so intent on replacing the plank that he paid little heed to Bill's words of wisdom. He lowered the flap door and, as the missing floorboard was a little to one side of the doorway, he used his plank to push the cattle out of the way. Then he tried to place the new board in position with his shunting pole. When the disturbed cattle started moving, one of them slithered and slipped, its hoof thrusting some rather liquid manure out through the doorway. Sailor was standing right in the target area and was splattered from cap to waistcoat, his face plastered.

He slammed the door shut, spitting and shouting at the disturbed beasts and roaring at Bill to get going. Bill and his mates were splitting their sides with laughter, but there was

Class 4F 0–6–0 No. 44520 of 2E (Saltley) at Westerleigh Yard.
(*c.* 1963 W.F. Grainger)

more to come. Soon they arrived at Westerleigh and shunted off the short train. As they were running light engine to Barrow Road shed, Sailor, still reeking, had to travel on the footplate. On the way, he asked Bill how to spell 'animal'. Bill asked, 'Why?' and was told, 'I believe I've swallowed some of that cow muck and I want to report it.' He showed Bill the draft of the note he intended to submit when going off-duty. Three times he had tried to spell 'animal', and each time he had spelt it differently, starting with 'any', 'eny' and 'anay'. This provided further amusement for Bill and his fireman. They were kind enough to correct it before they reached Bristol.

Rule 171(b) stated that 'guards working trains by which live stock is conveyed must carefully examine the animals from time to time, as may be necessary, and satisfy themselves that they are travelling safely; if any are found down and require attention, or otherwise require attention, steps must be taken to have them put right as soon as possible, and the circumstance recorded on the Guard's journal, the numbers of the vehicles and the sending and receiving stations being also given.'

'Crab' Class 5 2–6–0 No. 42900 of 2E (Saltley) at Westerleigh Yard.
(*c.* 1963 W.F. Grainger)

One night at Westerleigh a relief inspector was on duty. He was nicknamed 'Charlie Chaplin' owing to his rather splay-footed manner of walking. A train was on the point of departure from the Down sidings when the guard notice an animal was down. He shouted and thumped the side of the cattle truck, but all to no avail. If the cow failed to rise, the wagon would have to be removed from the train and taken to the nearest cattle pen for unloading. This would have caused serious delay and a great deal of work, especially if it involved feeding the whole group of animals if they had exceeded a certain period of travel time. So it was 'all hands to the pump' to raise the beast on to all fours.

Shunters and guards tried every inducement in the their knowledge and vocabulary, but all to no avail. At last, Charlie Chaplin, being the smallest man there, was persuaded to clamber through the bars into the wagon, but still he could not entice the cow to rise. Driver George Bridgewater, watching the proceedings, suggested, 'Pour a drop or two of water in its ear-hole.' One tea can of cold water was duly brought to the cattle van and handed to the intrepid inspector.

Now the correct method of administering the uplifting dose was by using a small tin nailed to the end of a fairly long stick, the operator remaining safely outside the vehicle. Charlie Chaplin, snugly ensconced inside the wagon, duly tipped a drop or two into the cow's ear. George Bridgewater, still watching, offered more helpful advice: 'If you want to get that beast to move, tip in about a cupful.'

Charlie Chaplin, blind to the potential outcome, did as he was bid – and the results were dramatic. The cow quickly reared up. Startled, Charlie Chaplin ran for the rails and threw himself out of the wagon, making a spectacular exit to the great delight of the audience who were thoroughly enjoying this diversion, watching the novice inspector learning the tricks of the trade the hard way. As George Bridgewater sagely remarked, 'He'll learn in time.'

In November 1941 the Southern Railway lent Drummond 'K10' class mixed traffic 4–4–0s Nos 135, 137, 138, 388 and 389 to the LMS. Nos 137 and 138 were shedded at Gloucester and the others at Bristol. One Barrow Road driver, working a Down goods train with one of these borrowed engines, found to his horror when descending the gradient of 1 in 69 south of Fishponds that the weight of the train had overcome his brake power. Fortunately he had a clear road ahead, as, with the whistle blowing, he ran

The result of a runback at Barrow Road
Motive Power Depot.
(21.4.28 Author's collection)

A brake van being removed following the
runback.
(21.4.28 Author's collection)

right into St Philip's coal yard. A pile-up was avoided by quick-thinking staff in the yard who heard the whistle, ran to the runaway train and succeeded in dropping sufficient wagon brakes to stop it crashing into the blocks.

Fishponds Bank, like any other significant gradient, had always been a potentially dangerous place. Some fifteen years earlier a Class 1F open-backed cab 0–6–0T with twenty wagons of locomotive coal from Barrow Road yard stopped at the bridge over the GWR line to Filton; as there was no brake van to restrain them, the wagons ran back by gravity when the engine stopped. Unfortunately the coupling between the first and second wagons snapped and nineteen of them broke away and crashed into a Class 2P 4–4–0 stored on one of the shed's side roads. The debris was piled almost as high as the shed roof. Foreman Ted Longden rang the employment office to send fifty men to clear the wreckage. The chargeman's report belied the seriousness of the event for he submitted: 'While bringing coal from the Yard to Loco, 19 broke away and ran into Loco siding. Slight damage to one or two wagons.' It was something of an understatement, to say the least.

Chapter Six

DEVELOPMENTS AT BARROW ROAD SHED

Barrow Road shed passed through several phases while Bill Bagnall was stationed there. Long before his time the original shed had been situated on the east side of the line by Engine Shed signal-box and following closure for locomotive purposes the building was used for wagon repairs. Today the wheel has turned full circle and the shed is now part of Barton Hill Traction & Rolling Stock Depot. When Bill arrived at Barrow Road, the roundhouse-pattern shed had a 42ft-diameter turntable. This meant that a Class 2P 4–4–0 with a wheelbase of about 45ft had to be run over the table and then a special pair of chocks levered over the table rails to form an extension on which to reverse the tender.

It was a well-known fact that an engine would turn more freely if its tender was less than half-full. If an engine proved stubborn to turn, a shout of 'All hands to the table' was given. In 1927 the 42ft inside table was replaced by a vacuum tractor-type 60ft turntable. A serious drawback to this was that the new inside table reduced the length of the shed roads radiating from it. The 45ft outside turntable was provided for engines not requiring shed occupation and also provided a means to turn the Midland & North Eastern Joint Postal Stock coaches. All five of these vehicles had to be turned each morning as the apparatus for mail exchange while on the move was only fitted on one side of the coaches.

Boilers received a regular washout after a recognised distance – generally 5,000 miles. If the water was dirty it could cause priming and then an engine would require a washout well before its scheduled mileage had been completed. In later years softened water was used to reduce scaling and corrosion in boilers. A scumming arrangement was provided which was supposed to remove scum from the top of the water in the boiler and then exhaust it into the ashpan when the engine reached a pressure point somewhere in the region of its maximum. This blowdown valve was fitted on the back plate of the firebox, and drained continuously a small quantity of water from the boiler when the regulator was open or the injectors were working. This kept down the concentration of soluble salts in the boiler water and so minimised priming.

The final phase of Barrow Road shed was the erection in 1938–9 of a hopper to hold coal in two 75-ton bunkers, an ash-handling plant and the removal of the outside turntable. The workshop was modernised and a running overhead crane of 70-ton capacity installed. The shop was also equipped with a wheel lathe and milling machine. A wheel-drop permitted a pair of wheels to be easily removed from an engine, replacing the previous laborious method of raising an engine by means of sheer-legs. The new arrangement meant that even a hot axle box could be removed, allowing its white metal recesses to be heated, remetalled and machined within a couple of hours. During the

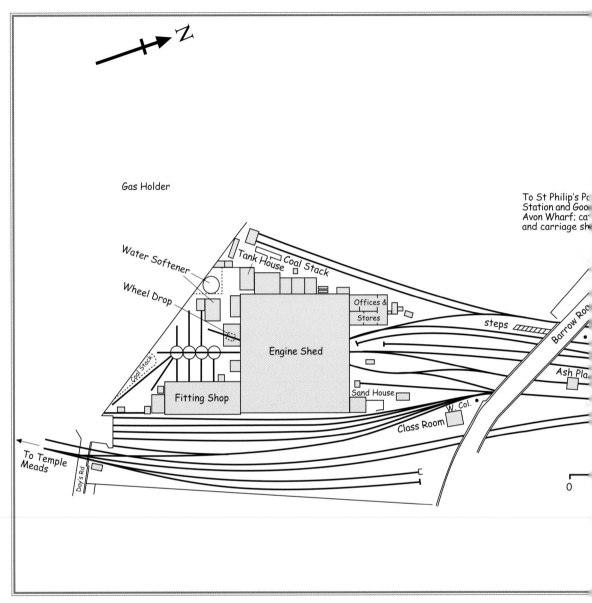

Plan of Bristol, Barrow Road, Motive Power Depot, 1939.

British Railways era, which brought a closer link with the ex-GWR Bristol locomotive depots, a 'Hall' class 4–6–0 with hot axle box trouble was sent to Barrow Road for attention. After placing the engine correctly over the wheel drop, the two Western Region men were invited to the cabin for a cup of tea. Meanwhile, it took the Barrow Road men only about 15 minutes to drop the wheels and take the set to the workshop. The fitter and his mate dismantled the axle box and the overhead crane moved it to the furnace where the old metal was melted out. The axle journal was examined and

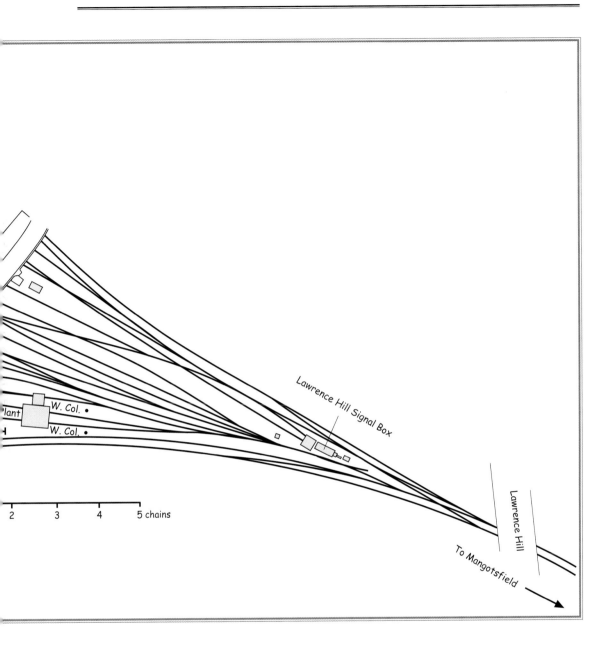

measured to determine the size of the new bearing. The St Philip's Marsh driver and fireman were loath to leave, so stayed and watched as the axle box cooled, was remetalled, rebored and then placed in the milling machine. The measured copy was inserted in the controls at the side of the miller and in half an hour the axle box was removed for the first test. A little more side skimming was done until the fitter was quite satisfied that it was an 80–90 per cent rub. Highly precise micro-engineering was inappropriate in this situation.

Bristol Barrow Road MPD, with BR Standard Class 3 2–6–2T No. 82040 on the left, and 'Jubilee' Class
4–6–0 No. 45649 *Hawkins* in the centre. In the background is the mechanical coaling plant.
(August 1964 W.F. Grainger)

The wheel set was returned to the wheel drop, raised to the engine's framing and
secured. Bill related that when the driver returned with the engine to St Philip's Marsh
shed, his foreman asked why he had brought it back – and was completely flabbergasted
to learn that the job was already done. In fact, he did not believe it until he examined it
himself. He then said, 'That's the last time anything goes to Barrow Road. We'll all be
out of work at this rate. The Midland taking just a few hours against our two days makes
a mockery of our set-up!'

Bill could never understand the peculiarities of GWR men and their extraordinary
belief that they, and only they, were 'enginemen', while those working for other
companies were merely 'drivers'. Bill vividly recalled an occasion when working a Class
4F 0–6–0 station pilot with his mate Dennis Coates. They were on the afternoon shift,
'tripping', that is, running coaches to and from Temple Meads. One of their duties was
to attach a van to a GWR express passenger train from Exeter at Platform 9. The van
behind Bill's engine was to be placed behind two others at the head of this express.
Normally GWR men were not expected to shunt, but allowed another engine to do the

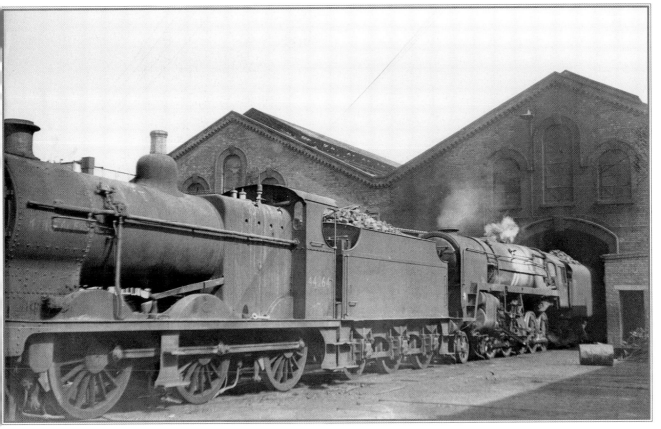

Class 4F 0–6–0 No. 44264 at Barrow Road.
(July 1963 W.F. Grainger)

shunting before they backed on. One particular week the shunter 'cut off' behind the two vans; then the GWR engine and two vans would draw forward so that Bill could place his van on the train in the correct position, third from the front. The GWR engine and its two vans would then reverse on to its train and in due course depart. This happened for three days. On the fourth afternoon an extra van had to be picked up at Temple Meads. To save an additional movement, the shunter decided that the GWR engine should collect the extra van. To say that the GWR man was vexed would be putting it mildly.

Around this time there was talk of the fact that a laser had been used at Swindon to test the wearing qualities of some engines, and that flaws had been found in the axles of a couple of 'Castle' class 4–6–0s. Now it was a 'Castle' which the Exeter man was driving. When his engine with the van drew alongside Bill he gave him a look that almost melted the paint. Bill decided to stir things up a bit and so addressed his fireman in a loud and carrying voice, 'Here you are Dennis, there's one of those "Castles" that fall to bits if they go over 60 miles an hour.' The result was electrifying. The GWR man yelled at Bill,

A busy scene at Barrow Road: the old manual coaling stage is on the left, with the main lines to the right.
(*c.* 1934 Author's collection)

'You, on that thing called an engine, I expect it's got a job to get to Fishponds with five 8-wheel coaches!' Bill replied, 'Get along with you, I was talking to my fireman, not you. I hope you manage to get to Bath!' Bill knew that the Exeter man worked to London and then lodged before returning.

Bill was certainly able to give as good as he got. One summer Saturday he was waiting with a Class 4P 4–4–0 Compound at Marsh Junction, Bristol, to take over a Paignton to Derby train of returning holidaymakers. Driving a Compound required knowledge of the regulator which was a dual opening affair. The first half of the quadrant admitted steam from the boiler to the two outside 21in-diameter cylinders, thereby creating power which was called 'simple engine'. The second half of the quadrant admitted steam to the 19in-diameter high-pressure cylinder and closed the opening which had provided steam for the two 21in cylinders. The steam now did its work via the 19in cylinder and exhausted into the low-pressure receiver which fed the two 21in cylinders. The steam was thus used twice, or 'compounded'. In the corner of the fireman's side of the cab a pressure gauge gave the reading of the low-pressure receiver, and when working compound this gauge usually gave a reading of 60lb psi. Once a Compound got into its

Barrow Road shed, with Class 2P 4–4–0 No. 520 on the right and Class 3P 4–4–0 No. 771 on the left. The old coaling stage, which was used until the mechanical plant was installed, is on the far left.
(*c.* 1934 S. Miles Davey)

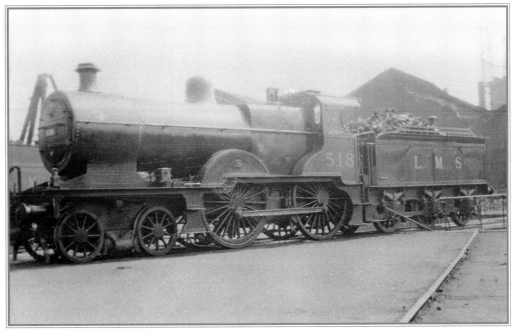

Class 2P 4–4–0 No. 518 by the outside turntable at Barrow Road.
(20.6.32 Colin Roberts collection)

BR Standard Class 3 2–6–2T No. 82038 under the ash plant at Barrow Road.
(April 1964 W.F. Grainger)

The interior of Barrow Road shed, with engines around the turntable. Left to right: Class 4F 0–6–0
No. 3858; Class 4P Compounds Nos 1026 and 1028; an unidentified Compound with extended and
strengthened front frames; Class 3P 4–4–0 No. 748; and Class 4F 0–6–0 No. 3875.
(c. 1936 S. Miles Davey)

Class 5 4–6–0 No. 45260 at Barrow Road with its rear set of driving wheels removed.
(1963 W.F. Grainger)

stride, travelling at 75–90mph was easy and it was comparatively comfortable on the footplate.

Before the train from Paignton arrived, a GWR driver boarded the LMS Compound and said, 'I'm to pilot you to Yate.' Bill said that it was unnecessary as he knew the road. But the GWR man pleaded not to be sent back and so Bill agreed that he should ride. Ten coaches arrived via the Relief Line which avoided the train having to stop at Temple Meads station, always congested on a summer Saturday. After Bill had seen that the coach vacuum reservoirs were corrected from 25 to 21lb psi, off they set over North Somerset Junction, Dr Day's Bridge Junction, and hard at it in Compound mode through Lawrence Hill station. When Stapleton Road distant was sighted as 'clear', the pilotman told Bill, 'You can go for it now', meaning he could open the regulator as a clear road was assured.

This was Bill's chance to tease his GWR visitor. Bill already had her in Compound, but with the regulator drawn back. On hearing the GWR man's words, he opened his

Class 4F 0–6–0 No. 44569 as station pilot at Temple Meads.
(16.5.64 Author)

regulator to the left-hand quadrant – that is, full opening at compound – and they laboured through Lawrence Hill and up the 2-mile long 1 in 75 bank. When they were passing through Horfield and nearly at the summit, the engine, still in compound, was finding it hard going. The GWR driver, most concerned at the labouring LMS engine, said, 'You'd better give her the lot on the rack.' Bill replied, 'I have, see,' and with his finger the visiting driver felt down the rack to the cut-off pointer. 'Good gracious, we ought to have had a banker! She's on full regulator and she ain't no stronger than a decent-sized cat.' Bill looked at his mate Den Coates and dared him to explain that Bill still had 'simple engine' to fall back on. Bill took the challenge of his engine being compared with a cat and hoped she would top the incline without him having to reveal the secret of the regulator valve.

They curved round through Stoke Gifford and gained LMS metals at Yate. Bill placed the cut-off at four notches and gradually reduced the regulator until 60lb psi showed on the low-pressure receiver indicator indicating that the engine was in complete balance.

Class 4P 4–4–0 Compound No. 1075 with the Down 'Devonian' passing the flyover near Yate South Junction.
(10.5.35 S. Miles Davey)

She now really began to speed. Bill estimated that they did over 80mph through Wickwar and Charfield which was normal with the regulator almost closed, the large port holding its position. The GWR pilot was now really impressed at the ease and speed at which they were travelling. As they ran into Gloucester he showed praise for the Compound by commenting, 'I'm pleased I stayed on and didn't get off at Yate. I saw what these engines can do. They ain't very strong but, blimey, they can certainly cover the ground!'

Bill remembers another incident when GWR men showed their superiority. Around 1937 half a dozen LMS men were sent to learn the road from Bristol to Weston-super-Mare so that they could work through trains to and from that resort and avoid engines having to be changed at Bristol, always a very busy place on a summer Saturday. Any way of speeding up working was welcomed. Three LMS men caught an early train to Weston and the one they returned on ran non-stop from Temple Meads to Paddington, but called at Yatton between Weston and Bristol. The LMS men tossed to determine who would travel on the footplate as the GWR driver only allowed one 'rider'. They even offered to fire so that the GWR fireman could ride on the cushions, but the GWR

A cab view of an unidentified ex-GWR 0–6–0PT waiting at Yate South Junction for a Bristol to Gloucester train to pass.

(*c.* 1963 W.F. Grainger)

driver almost foamed at the mouth: 'A Midland man firing on the Great Western – never!'

Bill was the third man to ride on the engine. Reg Ridout and Art Whitaker, who had ridden in the cab on the two previous days, had warned Bill about the unfriendly attitude of the GWR driver. As Bill was about to climb on the footplate he said, 'Wait a min', my mate has to see to the fire.' Bill carefully restrained himself on hearing this unfriendly greeting. After a brief firing, the driver said, 'You can get up now.' Before they left Weston, the driver twice directed the fireman, whom Bill assessed as being experienced and not needing advice, to 'Give her a couple over the front.' Bill noticed that the water and steam pressure were correct and could not understand his concern. Trying to break the ice, Bill asked, 'Is she a poor steamer?' 'All our engines steam well' came the snapped reply. Then the guard waved them off. As they travelled to Worle the fireman shovelled a couple of rounds and the driver opened the door for him. Bill commented further, 'This one seems an exception, doesn't it – your mate having to work like that?'

For a moment Bill thought the driver was going to stop there and then and order him off the footplate. When they called at Yatton, silence reigned on the locomotive. As they left the station the driver remarked, 'This is a London express.' 'Ah,' Bill replied. Anxious to get in another dig, he went on, 'but only from Bristol where you get off.'

As they passed Yatton East signal-box, the signalman there noticed a door not properly secured and so sent to Claverham signal-box the 'Stop and Examine' bell code, whereupon Claverham immediately threw all the Up signals to Danger. Now Claverham's distant signal was on the same post as Yatton East's starter and when they had run over the ATC [Automatic Train Control] ramp the bell indicated 'All Clear', but now, of course, Claverham's home signals were on. When Bill saw that the GWR driver was not going to stop at the home signals, he said, 'Ain't one of those signals ours?' Although the GWR driver was staring out of his window, the fact that he was approaching a signal at danger had not registered because he was relying on the ATC bell. As soon as Bill spoke, the driver whistled, dropped sand and braked, yelling, 'I had the bell! I had the bell!' Bill said, 'You were looking at the home signal and didn't notice it. If that's what the bell does, then I don't think much of it.' When they stopped, the fireman got down to inspect the train with the guard. He returned with the news that the suspect door handle had mysteriously righted itself and they proceeded to Temple Meads without further incident. Bill never forgot the look he received as he left the footplate at Bristol, the driver saying, 'I'll never allow a Midland driver on my engine again.' Hearing this, Bill then let fly with the full force of his pent-up indignation: 'I ain't a Midland man, I was LNWR, then LMS, but the Midland ran their trains on eyesight of signals, not on some new-fangled bell racket!'

On one occasion Bill was required to report on being 6 minutes late with the 5.00pm express coaching stock from Barrow Road carriage sidings to Temple Meads station. Bill was the driver of the tripper engine which moved stock from the sidings to the station and *vice versa*. On this occasion he had been in the sidings coupled to the coaches; beside him was another engine and stock, while the yard shunting engine was nearby. Thus, when the signal was pulled off, it could have applied to either train, or even for the yard shunter to go out on the main line.

Bill knew Rule 48(b) which stated: 'When a signal applies to more than one siding and more than one engine is in the sidings, a Driver must not move towards the signal so as to foul any other siding until he has been instructed to do so by the person in charge of the shunting operations.' Thus Bill correctly waited for the man in charge of the sidings to indicate who had to leave. As this person was in the shunters' cabin, there was a delay of some minutes before Bill received the hand signal that the road was his. But because Bill correctly waited in the siding, this delayed the 4.48pm fully-fitted express goods, which was a tobacco train to the north, and this in turn delayed the 5.00pm express.

In his report Bill wrote that 'not having a watch' he could not say how many minutes the siding signal was off before he received the hand signal as per Rule 48(b). Head

Class 5 4–6–0 No. 44836 on the Up main line at Yatton, probably returning to Bristol after heading a train to Weston-super-Mare.
(2.6.63 M. Wathen)

office, which dealt with the report, was greatly concerned about his 'not having a watch' so he was questioned by an inspector. Bill replied, 'Where in the rules does it say that I must have a watch?' The answer was that there was no such stipulation.

In 1962 Bill became a tutor driver for both steam and diesel traction and in 1966 retired on a weekly railway pension of 9s 9d.

Chapter Seven

BOB FORD MOVES FROM MAIN LINE TO THE GAS WORKS LINE

Because of stomach ulcers, Bob Ford had to leave British Railways in 1954, but he did not stop working on locomotives as he managed to secure a job driving a shunting engine at Bath Gas Works. There were two engines there: a Peckett 0–4–0ST No. 1267, built in 1912, and an Avonside Engine Company machine of the same wheel arrangement, No. 1978 of 1928. The Peckett's brakes were applied by turning a wheel – a frustrating arrangement for a shunting engine when it needed almost constant turning, a handle being a much easier design to operate.

Bob also drove rail-mounted steam cranes at Bath Gas Works. There were two of these. One was built in Macclesfield by Taylor Hubbard and was a smallish crane, capable of lifting 5 tons deadweight. The larger crane, with a tare weight of about 45 tons, was built locally by Stothert & Pitt of Bath and could also raise 5 tons. It was powered by two vertical pistons driving a wheel and everything operative received power from the main central shaft by means of cogs, including motive power for travelling or shunting wagons. Its vertical boiler had a working pressure of about 140lb and was no trouble to keep in steam.

The cranes were principally used for piling coal in stacks as reservoirs against any shortfall in supply owing to strikes, a shortage of railway wagons, disruptions caused by severe weather, or holidays. Space was at a premium, the works site being crammed in between the BR line, the River Avon and the Upper Bristol Road, with coal actually being stacked on some of the gas company's railway tracks. On days when the incoming supply was insufficient to cope with demand, the cranes transferred coal from those stacks to wagons. The small crane was often out of use, the large one being generally sufficient to handle all work unless demand was extreme. Both cranes were fitted with grabs which could be detached to turn them into ordinary lifting cranes. The Stothert & Pitt crane could lift perhaps 2–2½ tons of coal a one grab, eight or nine grabfuls loading a normal wagon. Unloading was a little less straightforward, care having to be taken to avoid damaging the wagon, particularly its floorboards. Getting the last hundredweight or so out required the assistance of a man who climbed into the wagon and shovelled the coal into one spot. Recovering coal from the corners was the greatest problem. Coal came from Somerset and from the Midlands, and in winter the works used up to 600 tons daily. The horizontal retorts were emptied and recharged by means of a ram which pushed the coke out on one side before coal was blown in.

Each block of retorts needed replacement every four years, this task being carried out in summer when gas demand was lower. Lifting the new retort sleeves from the railway

Bob Ford on the footplate of Bath Gas Works No. 1.
(*c.* 1958 Author's collection)

wagons they arrived in was a ticklish job for the cranes. Each sleeve, about 9ft in length and weighing 12–15cwt, was made of fireclay and so delicate it would crack like a duck's egg. A rope sling was secured to the crane's hook and carefully placed round the sleeve which arrived supported in such a manner that the sling could slide in beneath it. The crane lifted it to within about 3ft of the wheel at the top of the crane's jib, itself lowered considerably because weight was no problem at this range. The crane outside the retort house was required to travel forward, at the same time slewing its jib which had to enter a glass-less window, about 9ft high and 5ft wide. The sleeve had to be threaded through this relatively small aperture, together with the crane jib, without damaging the top arch of the window or fouling it; then it had to travel forward inside for a distance of perhaps another 10ft. To carry out this manoeuvre the crane started off with the sleeve in front of

Bath Gas Works engines. On the right is No. 1, Peckett Works No. 1267, built in 1912; on the left is No. 2, Avonside Works No. 1978, built in 1928. Note the severe track curvature.
(21.3.59 Ivo Peters)

A Bath Gas Light & Coke Company wagon, built by the Gloucester Carriage & Wagon Company and painted lead colour.
(January 1905 Author's collection)

In the foreground the eastern gas holder is under
construction at Bath Gas Works, using a Stothert &
Pitt rail-mounted crane.
(*c*. 1920 Author's collection)

it at right angles to the building, and by the time it was in position and the sleeve in
through the window the crane had moved about 15ft along the rails, continuously
slewing. From the moment the jib entered the window, the crane driver was unable to
see the retort, all movement being indicated by hand signals. It was all too easy to crack a
retort sleeve and then it had to be taken out again.

Thus Bob Ford learned and employed different driving skills from those required for
main line trains and the environment, too, was complete contrast. Instead of being
largely rural as it was when driving expresses on the main line, the gas works railway was
in distinct industrial surroundings, far from the clean air and scents of the countryside.
Bob's working life on the railway came to an end with the introduction of North Sea gas
to Bath and the consequent closure of the redundant Bath gas works in May 1971.

LOCOMOTIVE ALLOCATIONS TO BRISTOL AND BATH SHEDS, 1945

22A, BRISTOL, BARROW ROAD SHED, 1945

Class 3MT 2–6–2T 174
Class 2P 4–4–0 499, 553, 601
Class 4P 'Compound' 4–4–0 935, 1025, 1028, 1030, 1046, 1053, 1058
Class 1P 0–4–4T 1389, 1397
Class 1F 0–6–0T 1706, 1874, 1876
Class 2F 0–6–0 3090, 3094, 3517
Class 3F 0–6–0 3178, 3180, 3181, 3204, 3228, 3419, 3436, 3439, 3444, 3464, 3593, 3712, 3727
Class 4F 0–6–0 3853, 3928, 3953, 4112, 4135, 4169, 4411, 4422, 4424, 4466, 4534, 4535, 4536
Class 5MT 4–6–0 4804, 4805, 4812, 4843, 5272
Class 5XP 'Jubilee' 4–6–0 5557 *New Brunswick*, 5590 *Travancore*, 5612 *Jamaica*, 5618 *New Hebrides*, 5622 *Nyasaland*, 5627 *Sierra Leone*, 5629 *Straits Settlements*, 5652 *Hawke*, 5657 *Tyrwhitt*, 5665 *Lord Rutherford of Nelson*
Sentinel 0–4–0T 7190
Class 3F 0–6–0T 7544, 7550, 7678
Class 0F 0–4–0ST 11212

22C, BATH SHED, 1945

Class 3MT 2–6–2T 115, 181
Class 2P 4–4–0 497, 518, 696, 697, 700
Class 1P 0–4–4T 1324, 1334, 1348
Class 3F 0–6–0 3734
Class 4F 0–6–0 3875, 4096, 4102, 4402, 4523, 4557, 4558, 4559, 4560, 4561
Class 5MT 4–6–0 4844, 5056, 5440
Sentinel 0–4–0T 7191
Class 3F 0–6–0T 7275, 7316, 7465, 7496, 7542, 7557
Class 0F 0–4–0ST 11202
Class 7F 2–8–0 13800, 13801, 13802, 13803, 13804, 13805, 13806, 13807, 13808, 13809, 13810

Appendix II

SYLLABUS OF EXAMINATION OF ENGINE CLEANERS AND FIREMEN TO ACT AS FIREMEN AND DRIVERS RESPECTIVELY

B.R. 7070

**BRITISH TRANSPORT COMMISSION.
BRITISH RAILWAYS.**

EXAMINATION OF ENGINE CLEANERS AND FIREMEN
TO ACT AS FIREMEN AND DRIVERS RESPECTIVELY.

1. Training of Engine Cleaners in the duties of a Cleaner.

A Cleaner will be given practical instruction in the correct method of cleaning locomotives and the use of the various cleaning materials and tools.

2. Training of Engine Cleaners in the duties of a Fireman.

A Cleaner prior to being passed to act, when required, as a Fireman will be given preliminary tuition lasting two weeks by a Firing Instructor. This training will include instruction in :—

(a) Parts and functions of locomotives.

(b) Lighting, making up, cleaning and disposing of fires.

(c) Working of injectors and function of fusible plugs.

(d) Rules and regulations.

(e) Prevention of accidents.

(f) Coupling and uncoupling and general duties and responsibilities of a Fireman.

3. Passing of Engine Cleaners to act as Firemen.

In normal circumstances, no Cleaner will be allowed to act as Fireman on a locomotive until he has attained the age of 18 years, although there are certain temporary exceptions.

When an Engine Cleaner required for firing duties has been satisfactorily reported on by the Firing Instructor, he will be given an oral examination in the following subjects :—

(a) General description of a locomotive, i.e. names of component parts, etc.

(b) General knowledge of rules and regulations, particularly applicable to—
Hand and fixed signalling.
Protection of trains and opposite lines.
Locomotive equipment.

(c) Method of firing a locomotive and general duties and responsibilities of a Fireman.

An Engine Cleaner who fails, at the first attempt, to pass this examination to act as Fireman will be allowed two further attempts at stipulated intervals.

An Engine Cleaner qualified to act as a Fireman will be re-designated Passed Cleaner.

4. Promotion of Engine Cleaners or Passed Cleaners to Firemen.

Vacancies for Firemen will be filled in accordance with the provisions of the promotion arrangements agreed with the Trade Unions.

5. Passing of Firemen to act as Drivers.

No man is eligible to act as a Driver until he has been appointed Fireman, has attained 23 years of age and has performed 574 firing turns of duty.

When a Fireman is required for driving duties he will undergo a technical examination which will comprise an oral and practical examination.

(a) **Oral Examination.**

The candidate will be examined in the following subjects :—

(i) Knowledge of locomotive.

(ii) Knowledge of mechanism of continuous brakes.

(iii) Method of dealing with locomotive defects.

(iv) Knowledge of rules and regulations.

(v) Knowledge of the various types of signals, their use and the rules relating to the reading of signals.

(vi) Knowledge of the making out of reports.

(b) **Practical Examination.**

This examination will be carried out on the footplate of a locomotive in traffic.

Particular attention will be paid to the following points :—

(i) Care and manipulation of locomotive.

(ii) Attention to boiler and fire.

(iii) Attention to signals and judging distances.

(iv) Attention to rules and regulations.

(v) Knowledge of locomotive parts.

(vi) Making and using trimmings.

(vii) Care in and attention to oiling.

(viii) Examining locomotive and reporting defects.

(ix) General knowledge of automatic and steam brakes.

(x) Ability of examinee to change a boiler water gauge glass.

The practical examination is not to be carried out on the same day as that on which the oral examination is held.

A Fireman who fails to pass the technical examination to act as Driver at the first attempt will be allowed two further attempts at stipulated intervals.

A Fireman qualified to act as Driver will be re-designated Passed Fireman.

6. Promotion of Firemen or Passed Firemen to Drivers.

Vacancies for Drivers will be filled in accordance with the provisions of the promotion arrangements agreed with the Trade Unions.

7. Physical and Visual Examinations by Medical Officers.

Before being passed to act in a higher grade or on promotion to a higher grade employees are required, under the arrangements currently in force, to pass the physical and visual examination by the Medical Officer

INDEX

Figures in italics refer to illustrations